Also by Poppy Z. Brite

Exquisite Corpse

Lost Souls

Drawing Blood

Wormwood
(also published as *Swamp Foetus*)

Love in Vein
(editor)

Love in Vein 2
(editor)

COURTNEY LOVE

the real story

POPPY Z. BRITE

◇

simon & schuster

SIMON & SCHUSTER
Rockefeller Center
1230 Avenue of the Americas
New York, NY 10020

Designed by Sam Potts

Manufactured in the United States of America

1   3   5   7   9   10   8   6   4   2

Library of Congress Cataloging-in-Publication Data
Brite, Poppy Z.
Courtney Love : the real story / Poppy Z. Brite
p.   cm.
1. Love, Courtney, 1965–   .
2. Rock musicians—United States—Biography.   I. Title.
ML420.L872B75   1997
782.42166′092—dc21
[B]   97-35819
CIP
MN
ISBN 0-684-84506-7

ACKNOWLEDGMENTS

Without the help and kindness of Buddy D. Aaron, Carlene Bauer, Robin Bradbury, Nesta Brinkley, Connie Brite, Jennifer Caudle, Brian Celler, N. Cox, Richard Curtis, Christopher De-Barr, Paula Earley, Emmy from Texas, David Ferguson, Forrest Jackson, Curly Jobson, Caitlin R. Kiernan, L. Martin, Roberto Martinez, Dan Matthews, Dean Matthiesen, Amy V. Meo, Jenn Merino, D. Michel, Mary Ann Naples, Craig Nelson, Caroline Oakley, Robert Sage, Lucy Shanks, sources who wish to remain anonymous, Everett True, Laura Tucker, James T. Volker, Elizabeth Wang, and Ursula Wehr, this book would not be in your hands today.

For Abby, Annabel, Boris, Charlie, Colm, Crystal,
Gideon, Marcel, Marie, Nathan, Nicky, Rexina, Sredni Vashtar,
Todd, and Tomás, with love.

C O U R T N E Y   L O V E

There is a hole that pierces right through me.

—Euripides,
Medea

I'm a Courtney Love fan because I think she's a woman who goes beyond the limits of anything to say what she wants to say and to do what she wants to do. I think she's been through hell and back, and she's *survived!*

—Holly from
Salt Lake City
to Kevin Sessums,
Vanity Fair,
June 1995

I've seen your revulsion
And it looks real good on you

> —Courtney Love,
> "Teenage Whore"

Courtney Love calls me one night. I don't question how she got my unlisted number; people like her have Ways. She's in New Orleans; she liked my novel *Lost Souls;* do I want to go do some- thing? I invite her over. She arrives three and a half hours late, flops down on my couch with her legs sprawled out, drinks half a Diet Coke, and fills my living room with crackling energy and rapid-fire conversation.

She wears a black vintage dress, black hose, strappy high- heeled asskicker shoes. Her eyes are a startling sea-foam green, very large and very clear. She chain-smokes, but refuses our joint ("I can't smoke pot"). She is clear-eyed, friendly, and extremely articulate. She rules the room.

When we go out to a Cajun restaurant on Decatur Street with our assorted boyfriends, Courtney plugs an hour's worth of songs into the jukebox. Some gloomy old British stuff: Siouxsie, Echo and the Bunnymen. Lots of R.E.M.; she loves Michael Stipe. We try to convince her to have the excellent rabbit and sausage jambalaya, but Courtney says she can't eat bunny. She doesn't like the seafood gumbo she orders instead.

Toward the end of the meal, another diner approaches our table. Courtney sort of huddles into herself. The woman does not address Courtney, but points a finger at her and says to Courtney's date, "She looks *just like* Courtney Love!"

"Uh, she's not," he says politely.

The woman retreats. A minute later she returns and actually taps him on the shoulder. "You answered that so *fast*—almost like you were used to saying it!"

Courtney speaks. "It's just that I get it all the time and it gets annoying."

Now the woman is insulted. The date tries to distract her, asking what she does for a living. Turns out she's a tourist from New Jersey in town for some convention. "I'm just a *normal person,* the kind who pays *rock stars' salaries*—"

"I'M A STRIPPER, I DON'T GET A SALARY. WOULD YOU PLEASE GO AWAY?"

Our waitress intervenes, steers the irate fan away from the table, comes back and asks if we want her to slap the bitch around. We decline, but leave her a big tip.

Outside, Courtney leers at me. *"Welcome to my nightmare!"*

For her, it is the tip of a large and treacherous iceberg. For me, it's a revelation.

At one point while we were still in my apartment, Courtney upended her purse looking for something. I find two items of makeup under my couch later: a Poppy eyeshadow in Mushroom and a MAC lipstick in Diva. There are no coincidences.

When I get what I want then I never want it again

—Courtney Love,
"Violet"

1997

I finish this book. It wasn't her idea, but obviously having Courtney as a friend made the researching of it easier. It did not, however, make the *writing* any easier. In fact, I found it somewhat unnerving having a character who might actually call me up while I was writing about her.

During the course of my work, Courtney went through a great many changes in her public and private life. She was only a couple of years older than I, and I knew *I* still had plenty of growing up to do; I didn't expect her to stay static. But when you're writing a biography of a living, very active, extremely visible character, it can be hard to know where to stop.

Courtney Love has always been surrounded by chaos, triumph, pain, and glamour. Some of it has been beyond her control; some of it she has created herself, either unwittingly or deliberately. She has been presented as a gold digger, a saint, a cartoon character, a heroine, a martyr, and a role model.

In the media, Courtney has been dissected, analyzed, and stitched back up again. Her behavior, her sex life, her wardrobe, her music, her acting, and, most recently, her fashion sense and style have become topics of intense interest all over the world. She has been slapped (and has occasionally plastered herself) with numerous and conflicting labels: riot grrrl, rock star, feminist, antifeminist, drug addict, musical trailblazer, brave widow, slut, bitch, new Hollywood talent.

17

The purpose of this book is not to condemn or defend Courtney Love—everyone seems to feel obliged to do one or the other
—but to chronicle the first thirty-two years of her fascinating life
as accurately as possible.

◇

It was autumn in San Francisco, the season of the witch, 1964.

Somebody in the Haight was giving a party for jazz legend Dizzy

Gillespie, and Hank Harrison was invited. Hank believed himself

to have a standing invitation to any party in San Francisco,

whether anyone had actually invited him or not; his music con-

nections got him in everywhere.

Hank was going places. His old college buddy Phil Lesh

played bass with a hot band called the Warlocks, and Hank was always bragging that Phil could get him a gig in the music business anytime. He would later claim to have managed the Warlocks, who in 1965 would change their name to the Grateful Dead.

Heavy-set and round-faced, with a humped nose, a scruffy black mustache, and a hairline that was beginning to recede, Hank was nobody's pretty boy. But he was a loquacious charmer. His gift of gab and his music connections got him plenty of girls, and that night at Dizzy Gillespie's party, they got him Linda Risi.

Linda was a naive rich girl on her own for the first time. A San Francisco native, she had grown up on ritzy Nob Hill and gone to Catholic school. Now she was nineteen and adrift in the city, swayed by the burgeoning vibes of the sixties. Blonde and slender, neat and WASPish, she didn't blend into the Haight-Ashbury crowd. That was why she caught Hank's attention.

The adopted daughter of an optician (and an heiress to the Bausch optical fortune), raised in the Catholic church, Linda had come to San Francisco upon reaching her majority. Like so many other young people in that city, in that year, she was looking for something she couldn't identify or explain. She didn't find it in Hank Harrison, but for a while she thought she had. They left the party together that night, and staggered up and down the steep sidewalks of the magically lit, carnival-like Haight until they reached Hank's dingy apartment.

Linda was already pregnant when she married Hank in Reno a few months after they met. Hank kept feeding her a line about how the combination of their genes—his brains and her looks— would produce the perfect child. Linda had no way of knowing that half of Hank's genes came from a violently alcoholic father, and, being adopted, she knew nothing about her own genes. (Linda would later allegedly discover that her biological father had been a psychiatrist from New York, and his father had been a Jewish psychoanalyst from Vienna, but since she was a well-known therapist herself by the time of this "discovery," it must be taken with a grain of salt.)

Hank has since claimed that Linda refused to use birth control because of her religious beliefs. Whatever the case, Linda could not have given up the baby even if Hank had wanted her to. Her own adoptive father had been an abusive drunk, and Linda considered herself an outcast, a person with no family at all. This baby would be the first blood relative she had ever known.

Linda Harrison nurtured her fetus in a heady broth of fear and sugar: she constantly craved candy, cookies, any kind of sweets. She gained weight, vomited all the time, felt that pregnancy had made her hideously ugly. Hank, already getting bored with the relationship, did nothing to allay her fears.

At 9:15 A.M. on July 9, 1965, at St. Francis Memorial Hospital, Linda gave birth to a daughter whose birth certificate read Love Michelle Harrison. The labor had been long and wrenchingly painful. Linda tried to imagine what her baby must have felt, expelled from the cradling womb, constricted for hours in the tight tube of muscle. She imagined that the child had been frightened and furious, and had taken out every ounce of it on her.

Hank was not in attendance at the birth. Sleeping late after a Warlocks gig, possibly. Who knew? But Linda and the other freaks made an occasion of the birth anyway: Courtney would later claim that they had stewed Linda's placenta with onions and eaten it.

Linda, now twenty, adored her daughter helplessly. She had no idea how to care for a baby, though she was sure she had the good "instincts" of every hippie mama. That hungry pink mouth tugging on her heavy breasts, those fierce eyes staring up at her with disquieting awareness—these quickly became the most important things in Linda's life. No child ever had a needier mother, and the baby must have sensed the chasm of Linda's emotional dependence.

Even then, though, Linda's feelings toward her daughter were ambivalent. Love Michelle didn't always act like a normal baby. She did frightening things: stiffened and screamed upon being cuddled; cried until she all but passed out from lack of oxygen. A photograph taken of the Harrison family at Christmas 1965 shows Linda sitting stiffly with a strained smile on her pretty face, legs crossed at the knee, ignoring the arm Hank has draped around her shoulders; she is distinctly looking *away* from the baby and does not appear to be touching her. The baby has a lost look, and her hands are reaching toward Linda.

The Harrisons lived in a big Victorian house that Linda's parents had paid for. As well as supporting Hank, Linda often cooked for a ragtag assortment of musicians, groupies, and street urchins. The baby grew up in a fantasy world partly of her own design, partly sketched in by the freaks and artists around her. None of these happy hippie dreamers, though, suspected how dark the child's own inner world was. The earliest dreams she remembered were nightmares of skeletal wraiths, deformed internal organs, poisoned milk (the latter a motif that would recur in her poetry and her later songwriting).

Meanwhile, the people around her wanted her to "act like a flower," to "dance like springtime." She was encouraged to stretch her imagination, and occasionally was helped along with a bit too much zeal. When she was four years old, she has said, her father gave her LSD. (She has no memory of this, but later, during the Harrisons' divorce, Linda and one of Hank's girlfriends would testify that it was so in child-custody court.)

The effects of LSD on a four-year-old are difficult to speculate upon. LSD is best known for causing hallucinations, which may have been especially frightening to an already disturbed child. But LSD also causes introspection and heady flights of imagination. How different would the experience have seemed from her usual highly subjective reality? Did she have a bad trip, and what would a four-year-old's bad trip be like? Did she tap into some well of preconsciousness that adults could never hope to access? Did she even notice?

She has said that her father was involved in the manufacture and sale of LSD in those days, and that he may have supplied the Dead. If so, his acid was probably clean and pure. Though the experience can be psychologically damaging, LSD itself causes no physical harm to the brain or body. Perhaps she just saw colors and pretty lights; perhaps it was even a temporary escape from the confusion of her everyday life.

Although everything was supposed to be peace and love, her parents fought all the time and her father scared her. She was glad when Linda told her that Hank would be moving out for good.

Linda and Hank divorced in 1970, and both sued for custody of their daughter. In the ensuing trial, the charges of Hank's having dosed the child were brought out, and custody was awarded to Linda, who promptly changed her five-year-old daughter's first name to Courtney after a woman she'd known during her pregnancy. "Love" apparently no longer applied to the product of her union with Hank.

Soon after the divorce, Hank disappeared with a Deadhead girl and Linda married again. Love's father had been horrible, but it looked as if Courtney's stepfather might be a nice man.

Frank Rodriguez was a schoolteacher from Portland, and the organizer of that city's Kite Day. He talked to Courtney like a real adult talking to a real child, not in the unfiltered hippie psychobabble she was used to hearing. He also legally adopted her and gave her his surname. Frank was the first (and possibly the only) benevolent authority figure in her life. Tellingly, she began calling him "Daddy" as soon as he and Linda were married, and Hank became "BioDad."

"Courtney was a wonderful child," Frank told *Premiere* years later. "She had a strong will. There were things she didn't want to do. I wanted her to dress in saddle shoes. But she hated them. She wanted Mary Janes. We went round and round about that kind of stuff. Boy, she sure has gotten them now."

The Rodriguez family relocated to Eugene, Oregon, where Linda started attending psychology classes at the university. Soon she had decided psychological work was her true calling, and the entire family underwent therapy at her behest.

Linda and Frank had two daughters together, Jaimee and Nicole. With other children around, even babies, Courtney felt like the outcast again. Her behavior became increasingly moody, even violent. She made disturbing crayon drawings of terrible things happening to her baby half sisters. Linda apparently became resentful because coping with Courtney's problems began to encroach on her time with her two younger daughters. Linda and Frank were having problems, too. They both began seeing other people, and the marriage split up. Though Courtney would keep in touch with Frank, and her own daughter would eventually call him Grandpa, she must have felt that she was losing the only father she'd ever known.

He was soon replaced by David Menely, a sportswriter and outdoor-expedition leader Linda met on a river-rafting trip. She brought him home, married him, and asked him to adopt her daughters, giving Courtney her third surname in eight years.

David was not as nice as Frank. He had a cynical wit that Courtney admired—something she recognized in herself—but he could be vicious. He smoked pot constantly, but it didn't seem to mellow his acerbic personality any, and Courtney associated the smell of pot smoke with BioDad.

In 1973, the Menelys moved from Eugene to a nearby commune in Marcola, where they lived in what Courtney later described as a "tepee." It was a large hut with rough-hewn timbers and a packed-earth floor, full of smoke and shared by many other people. The commune discouraged gender "stereotyping," and Courtney was no longer allowed to wear girly clothes or play with dolls, not that she'd ever had many of either. As she had been in the San Francisco house, she was exhorted by the hippies around her to express herself and be creative.

But the commune's facilities were worse than primitive. Courtney still talks about how the kids at her school called her "Pee Girl" because no one ever thought to wash her clothes. The photograph on the back of her second album, *Live Through This*, dates from this period. It shows a little girl standing barefoot on a gravel road, her skin shockingly pale, her long hair golden-brown and stringy. Her plaid shirt is too large, and unbuttoned farther than might be considered appropriate for, say, a school picture. Her expression is indecipherable.

In school, Courtney had always performed poorly despite her obvious level of intelligence. Most of the other children shied away from her, and she from them. She was diagnosed by one of her therapists as mildly autistic. To Linda, Courtney seemed to be in pain most of the time: hating to be touched, seething with silent rages, withdrawing into a world where no one else could go. Linda knew something was wrong with her oldest daughter, but no one could tell her exactly what.

Now a well-known therapist, Linda recently broke her long-standing silence about her famous daughter to speak to *Vanity Fair*. "I think that Courtney came with a tremendous sense of pain in her," she told writer Kevin Sessums in 1995. "She's not any different than she was when she was two years old . . . yet there were times, even as a small child, she would be really, deeply touched by something. And when that would happen, it was as though every part of her went soft for a little while—including her heart.

"When she was in the second grade in Eugene, Oregon, she was having a lot of nightmares. I had no idea what to do. I took

25

her to a psychiatrist just to try to find some way to bring her some solace. The psychiatrist said part of the problem with her was that she needed to join Girl Scouts. She needed to be involved in ordinary kid activities. I dutifully went to a Brownies meeting with her . . . I could tell it was really hard for her to be in the same room with all these kids. The Brownies leader suggested they have an art show. She asked all the kids to draw something. The things that Courtney drew were always startling. She didn't draw sunsets and apple trees. She would draw sort of . . . *wounded figures*. I can still see her that day—her little face so intense with those crayons. At the end of that, the teacher told the troop that they were going to see what drawing they liked the most by holding them up one by one and everyone applauding. I knew that this would be terrible for her. When it got to hers, she just grabbed it and ran over to me, and we left.

"At that time, when a child was exhibiting the kind of pain Courtney was exhibiting—a lot of nightmares and a lot of crying and hating school and hating *everything*—the treatment was pretty much to try and make that child what they called 'normalized' rather than saying, 'What kind of creature is this, and how can we make her be okay with who she is?' That whole belief system was really awful for her."

Courtney's old friend Robin Bradbury offers a different perspective. "I don't know how much of it is true, but she told me stuff like they thought she was a bad influence on her sisters, so they would make her sleep in the shed, and they tried to have her put in a psychiatric place and they did some tests on her and found out that she had a genius IQ, but they [Linda and David] were trying to say she was crazy and keep her away from her sisters . . . She was a little kid, for God's sake. I just don't think they had time for her."

Courtney tells of auditioning for a school production of *Snow White* around this same time, certain that she was destined to play the lead. "I studied the part of Snow White forever and had it down," she recalls. "And they gave me, without even auditioning me, the part of the Evil Witch." It was clear that school was never going to be a happy experience for her.

When Courtney was eight, Linda and David Menely made the surprising decision to move to New Zealand and start a sheep ranch with Linda's Bausch money. It would be a fresh, uncluttered life, Linda thought. She and Courtney had begun to have hysterical fights about trivial matters, fights that sometimes made Linda feel younger and weaker than her own daughter. In keeping with her new, uncluttered life, she arranged to leave Courtney with a therapist friend back in the States.

Courtney escaped this abandonment by dreaming of fame, of a time when people would cry and swoon in her very presence. One day she made a clay model of herself and contemplated it with something approaching awe: *she* had absolute control over this thing, this icon of herself. But control was only a fantasy; in real life she had no say in where she lived, with whom she lived, or even how she was treated. She could mold and crush the clay doll just as the adults in her life could do to her.

School had become an active source of terror. Courtney dreamed about keeping tiny people in jars and starving them, about starting a farm for women where she would beat them and make them beautiful. She sneaked Dorals from the therapist friend's purse and invented witchy little rituals in her room. The friend had a son who called Courtney ugly and fat, then tried to do other things when no one was looking—grabbing at her, touching her with dirty fingers. Courtney sneaked into his bedroom one day, pricked her finger with a pin, and dabbed blood on his pillow. Soon afterward, the friend dispatched Courtney to her family in Nelson, New Zealand, on the north end of the southern island.

Even there, Courtney was too much trouble. Though Jaimee and Nicole were living with them on the ranch, Linda and David sent Courtney to stay with another friend. Shirley, though, was nothing like the therapist friend with the beastly son. She was a self-proclaimed spinster with a wonderful collection of books and a garden, and she acted as if she didn't mind having Courtney around, maybe even loved her a little. School in New Zealand wasn't as bad as it had been in the States. For the first time she could remember, Courtney let herself believe that her short, sad life was getting better.

But Linda came for a visit and everything went back to hell. Shirley, Linda claimed, had begged her to take Courtney away. Courtney was driving Shirley "crazy" and she "couldn't handle it." Courtney had no idea what she might have done to make Shirley so mad.

Was there any truth to Linda's claim? Shirley was a person who valued her privacy; she might well have found the sudden responsibility of caring for a young child overwhelming. Then again, Linda may have been jealous of her daughter's relationship with Shirley, which was obviously more important to Courtney than her relationship with Linda.

Whatever the reason, Courtney had to go live on the sheep farm with Linda and David. By this time they had adopted an emotionally disturbed boy. Courtney was not allowed to play with her siblings, and was forced to sleep alone in a tiny hut behind the main house. Courtney spent much of her time sitting in the pasture, daydreaming about being a witch, making little slits in her skin with sharp blades of grass until the blood ran down her inner arms.

Linda and David had a son. Courtney found the baby ugly, and thought he had a mean look. When her half brother got sick and died in the hospital before ever coming home, Courtney was afraid she would get blamed for the death somehow. Still, she couldn't help wishing all Linda's babies had died—all except her. Then Linda would have to love her.

"I feel like not being here all the time," Courtney told author Amy Raphael in 1994. "I've felt it since I was six or seven. I remember the first time it hit me. I was on a cliff in New Zealand.

But I never do anything about it because it's my responsibility not to. If I don't outgrow it in this lifetime, I'm not ever gonna outgrow it."

She had a long, long way to go.

CHAPTER TWO

◇

For Christmas 1975, David Menely gave his ten-year-old step-

daughter her first drink.

Linda had bought Courtney cheap, dull presents: pastel cray-

ons and oil paints while her half sisters got party dresses and

Mary Janes. Linda had always gone a little overboard urging

Courtney to be creative, but in Courtney's mind these presents

were a total denial of her own femininity. The alcohol brought

out all her resentment of her family. They weren't really her family, Courtney realized; no one was. She remembers screaming hysterically at them and seeing them all back away. At that moment she felt more like a monster than ever before.

Sometime during the night Courtney crawled into bed with Linda and huddled beside her. But when she woke up still drunk and started screaming again, her mother kicked her out of the bed, and Courtney staggered away. She awoke the next morning covered with mud and vomit in a paddock of the sheep farm. When she opened her eyes, she felt years older than she had when she'd last closed them. She knew then that her mother was never going to want her.

She was shipped back to the States to live with Frank Rodriguez and his new wife in Portland. As usual, the kids at school hated her. Most of them smoked pot, and Courtney felt weird whenever she did—even the smell reminded her of very early childhood, BioDad, Linda's distance. Courtney saw pot brownies in the fridge, but when she drank some sherry, Frank demanded that Linda take her back. Linda refused, sending her instead to Nelson College for Girls, an Anglican boarding school in New Zealand.

Courtney liked attending a Commonwealth school. The girl who had had so little structure in her life enjoyed the discipline of getting up at six A.M. and making her bed military-style. For the first time, she met other girls who weren't scared or repulsed by her. When some students got expelled for drinking vodka gimlets, Courtney worshiped them.

The school kicked her out—"for weirdness," she has said. The school's principal, Alison McAlpine, recently spoke to the press about her famous student. "It would be fair to say we didn't know of her existence until her rise to fame. We've been embarrassed by her in the last little while." Presumably, Nelson College girls are not meant to become loudmouthed celebrities.

Courtney was sent back to Eugene, where she stayed with one of Linda's ex-boyfriends, Michael, a therapist. Soon after starting

American school, she was moved ahead three grades. Apparently the Commonwealth discipline had done her good.

Linda, now separated from David Menely, soon returned to Oregon too. But Courtney stayed with Michael. She told *Melody Maker* in 1991,

> I came back from New Zealand and I had to go to this tough school. I didn't know anything about guys then, but I knew that you were supposed to desire them and they were better than horses or Sweet or the Bay City Rollers.
>
> I'd been at that school for a week and I was popular because I had this accent and I was into this Bowie thing. There was this guy and his name was Gary Graff and he was really nice to me and sweet and cool and funny, and followed me around and everything. So we went out to the place where everyone smoked and he kissed me and gave me this hickey on my neck.
>
> So then these two incredibly popular girls asked me where I got my hickey, and I was really proud, and I said, "Oh, this guy Gary Graff," and they started laughing and cracking up. The deal was that Gary Graff was the biggest geek in school and everybody made fun of him. I didn't want that to happen to me, so I ignored him. I did that to him.

By this time, Courtney had made up her mind that the bad crowd was her only hope. Michael always had loads of marijuana, so she would steal it and share it with the pothead kids who hung out at the Eugene mall. She got beaten up, but assumed that was a necessary peril of hanging out with the bad crowd.

When a store detective caught Courtney shoplifting a Kiss T-shirt from Woolworth's, Linda couldn't be found. Courtney was put in the "holding pen," a county reform school. While she was there, footage of her appeared on the local news. The staff wouldn't allow her into the TV room to see it, and Courtney ripped up a bedsheet in her fury. When her case came before the judge, the shoplifting charges were dropped, but she was found guilty of "criminal mischief" for destroying government property (the sheet) and sent to Skipworth, a maximum-security juvenile hall.

After performing a battery of IQ tests, psychiatrists decided that Skipworth wasn't the place for Courtney. Her sentence was commuted to two years' probation, which she soon violated by running away from home. This time she was sent to Hillcrest, an institution for criminally inclined eleven-to-eighteen-year-olds in Salem, Oregon.

Her only friend at Hillcrest was Geneva,[1] a girl she'd met briefly at Skipworth. Geneva was a chronic runaway, a creature as isolated and intense as Courtney herself. She'd been sexually abused by her father and had a habit of offering herself to anyone who showed her the slightest affection; at the same time she was fierce, with a dangerous beauty and a vicious tongue. The two girls used to sneak into each other's room at night and howl at the moon until some orderly came and dragged them off to the "Quiet Room."

Courtney not only saved her juvenile-hall records, she used them as stationery for years. A report dated November 17, 1978, states, "Courtney has 'motor mouth' trouble—it's working over-time—she verbally assails & abuses former cottage members—causes a continual disruption in class. Moreover her obscene expressions are not necessary & mostly derive from disgusting attitude rather than actual provocation. I cannot condone nor tolerate this behavior—I am taking steps to make sure it never happens again."

In May 1979, Courtney was placed in the foster care of one

---

[1] Not her real name.

Sally Johns in Portland. There is no record of why Ms. Johns could not keep the thirteen-year-old, but by September she was back at Hillcrest, where a report tells of her being dragged from her room and thrown into the Quiet Room for an unnamed infraction. Later the same month, a more interesting report was filed.

> Courtney had permission to visit her father Hank Harrison on Sat. at 4pm. She returned from the Ad. Bldg. about 6pm. About 6:30 . . . students noticed a peculiar odor that they expressed was marijuana. All students were sent to their rooms. As Christa's[2] room was most odiferous her room was searched. A Baggie with a handful of marijuana was found in the closet. Christa said Courtney and she smoked a small amount in her room. (Neither student appeared disoriented so the nurse was not called.) Courtney denied smoking the marijuana on 1st questioning, although she admitted it later. She said she brought it on her person from the Ad. Bldg. as her father had given it to her.

Back to the Quiet Room, courtesy of BioDad.

Another Quiet Room report, dated only three days later, shows a different side of Courtney. "When I came on duty, Courtney was telling fairy tales to Janie.[3] When the story ended, they said Goodnight and went to sleep. No problems on my shift."

Yet another report, dated October 29, 1979, has been decorated by the adult Courtney with cutouts of a silver spoon, a naked woman, and the headline MADONNA—"I HAVEN'T GOT

---

[2] Not her real name.
[3] Not her real name.

AIDS"—BUT SHE WANTS TO SIGN HOLE TO HER NEW LABEL. It reads, hilariously, "Courtney and Susan⁴ had problems getting along this AM and almost came to blows. I had them go to their rooms to calm down. Courtney threw a cream sachet jar thru her window breaking it in tiny pieces which flew out in the hall."

A more ominous tale went into the file on November 11. "Courtney began screaming and swearing about bugs in her room at 11:00 PM. Refused to be reasonable. She became louder and more insistent. Coordinator was called and Courtney was escorted to Quiet Room . . ."

On January 30, 1980, Courtney came up for foster placement again, and her case was given a detailed examination by Hillcrest's Student Review Committee. This report is reproduced in its entirety.

REASON FOR HEARING

Courtney is being seen by the SRC to be considered for placement. Courtney was last seen by the Committee on December 5, 1979, for a regular review.

ACADEMIC PROGRAM
Courtney is enrolled as a full time student at Robert S. Farrell High School. She is presently in the tenth grade and in Mrs. Newton's core class in the mornings. Her afternoon classes include US History, drama, and studying in the Media Center.

Courtney's adjustment to the academic program at Robert S. Farrell has been excellent. She has maintained excellent grades throughout her entire stay

---

⁴ Not her real name.

at Hillcrest. Since Courtney arrived on Kappa Cottage in September, 1979, she has consistently done well academically. The previous school quarter which ended in November saw Courtney make honor roll status.

Behaviorwise, Courtney has had significant problems in the school program. She is a very intelligent young lady who tends to overextend herself as far as dealing with people in the school program. She is very outspoken and to the point of having or causing problems with the program because of her boisterous behavior. She has been sent back to the cottage on numerous occasions in the past months because of behavior problems in the school program.

Courtney's academic ability is seen to be far beyond the typical student at Hillcrest.

COTTAGE PROGRAM

Courtney has been involved in the GGI [Guided Group Interaction] program on Kappa Cottage since her arrival. There was an approximate six week session in which Courtney was removed from group because of her negative, hurtful behavior. This seems to have a definite effect on Courtney and when she returned to the group program, she handled the help sessions in a much more positive fashion. Courtney's major problem areas seem to be her low self image. Courtney does not feel that she is as strong as she appears to be. She puts up a very good ''front.'' While appearing to be very strong and capable externally, internally Courtney appears to be a very frightened young lady who has never met with very much success at anything that she has tried.

Courtney has made some progress in the area of improving her self concept; however, her anger and hurtful behavior toward others is still evidenced on cottage. It seems that at times, Courtney spends more energy trying to find ways to beat the system rather than trying to work within its confines to accomplish her own goals. This behavior pattern has been consistent in both the GGI groups and on the cottage behavior. Courtney is presently expressing some very severe feelings of fear regarding placement in the community.

MEDICAL AND PSYCHIATRIC

Courtney is presently in good physical health. She has been referred to Dr. Daly, consulting psychiatrist, and has been seeing him.

COMMUNITY RESOURCES

Placement planning for Courtney has been rather difficult. Her natural father, Hank Harrison, has made himself known to Courtney since her return to Kappa Cottage. She did spend Thanksgiving with Mr. Harrison in the San Francisco area. She returned from this visit and stated that she definitely did not want to live with Mr. Harrison. Courtney's mother and Courtney both indicated that she should not live at home with her mother. Her stepfather, Mr. Rodriguez, indicated that he is not willing to take Courtney home on placement. Since Courtney is due to be terminated in two months, this has placed a real burden in finding placement for her. Courtney has been accepted by the Hines group home in Corvallis, and is willing to make an effort to try the placement there. This seems to be the most appropriate placement since the

Hines home would be able to continue supervising Courtney even though she has been terminated from the juvenile system.

EVALUATION AND RECOMMENDATION

Courtney has not made a great deal of progress since she was placed on Kappa Cottage. This is Courtney's third try at graduating from a program here at Hillcrest. She seems to be more knowledgeable in GGI than most of her group members and tends not to get much help because she functions beyond their level. Courtney has been at Hillcrest for almost two years now and it is felt that since Courtney's return to the community with termination approaching rapidly, perhaps a low keyed living situation such as the Hines Home could provide the best resource for Courtney.

Courtney seems to have made some progress in her problem areas of low self concept, anger, and authority problems. Basically, Courtney is intelligent enough to know exactly what she needs to do in order to be successful in the community. It is a matter of whether Courtney is willing to invest her own time. One of the serious considerations is that Courtney has been at Hillcrest nearly two years and feels quite comfortable here. Since her termination is rapidly approaching, the idea was to place her in a parole setting in order that she may be able to make some satisfactory adjustment prior to her termination.

It is the recommendation of the Kappa Cottage team that Courtney be placed in foster care to the Hines Group Home, effective February 1, 1980.

FINDINGS

Courtney appeared before the Student Review Committee for placement consideration.

Courtney told the Committee that she felt she was
being kicked out of Hillcrest again. She feels she
has made some progress on her problem areas and is
being placed at the Hines Home.

Courtney feels this is a last-ditch effort to get
her out of the system. Courtney is close to termination and this is the only suitable placement that
seems appropriate. Courtney will be involved in a
tutoring program at the Hines Home.

ORDER

The SRC orders Courtney to be placed in foster care
at the Hines Group Home, 740 SW 57th, Corvallis, Oregon, effective Feb. 1, 1980.

Some sections of this report ("Courtney does not feel that she
is as strong as she appears to be. She puts up a very good 'front'
... Basically, Courtney is intelligent enough to know exactly
what she needs to do in order to be successful in the community")
accurately reflect Courtney's personality today. Some ("Courtney
appears to be a very frightened young lady who has never met
with very much success at anything that she has tried") show how
much work still lay ahead of her.

Courtney was placed at the Hines Home on February 1 and
ran away four days later. She remained missing until the twenti-
eth, when she called Hillcrest and asked if they could get her into
a place called the Looking Glass Shelter Home. They pulled
the necessary strings, but advised her that this placement was
"extremely temporary" since Looking Glass didn't want her.

The Looking Glass Shelter Home requested her removal on

February 29. Local Child Services denied Courtney use of their family shelter home. Confronted with these facts, Courtney agreed to return to Hines rather than have her parole revoked.

It is unclear how long she stayed this time, but she was definitely gone by April. A report from her parole officer dated April 9, 1980, states that "Courtney contacted this parole officer from California. She is staying with a young woman . . . who wants to provide a foster home for her . . . Mrs. [Linda] Menely agrees to accept Courtney on parole with permission to live elsewhere." Courtney's case was closed at Hillcrest on May 24, 1980.

Courtney was staying with Alex,[5] the cousin of Courtney's friend Julie,[6] another girl from Hillcrest. Julie, a manic, promiscuous fourteen-year-old, had run away to Alex's house in northern California. Courtney joined them for lack of anywhere better to go, smoked a lot of pot, and sat in the backs of Camaros listening to Journey. A teenage couple who also lived in the house spent most of their time screaming at each other.

Alex's boyfriend was a Hell's Angel who looked like Epstein from TV's *Welcome Back, Kotter.* His intelligence and sarcastic wit attracted Courtney, and the two of them spent hours in conversation, but she had no sexual interest in him. He had *facial hair,* for God's sake, and in many ways she still thought of herself as a child. But Alex didn't see it that way. Soon Alex was on the phone to her mother screaming about "nymphets," and Courtney was feeling increasingly unwelcome in yet another home.

Then she got a call from her old Hillcrest friend Geneva, she of the nights spent howling at the moon. Geneva had tracked her down somehow. "I need you," Geneva said, and began to cry. It was a strange feeling for Courtney to hear that she was needed. It was also the perfect excuse to get away from Alex's psychodrama.

Courtney broke her parole and ran away to Geneva's father's

[5, 6] Not their real names.

house in Springfield, Oregon. The house was a hovel, and Geneva's father was a pervert whom Geneva had seen masturbating outside her window.

They ran away to Geneva's grandfather's place in North Bend. Grandpa lived in a trailer park full of junkies, all of whom tried to fuck the girls. Soon they stole a bottle of Black Velvet whiskey and hitchhiked to Eugene, where Hank Harrison somehow managed to find Courtney. He offered to fly both girls to his place in Marin County, and they accepted. After the company they'd been keeping, even Hank was something of a comfort.

The first night in Marin County, Geneva and Courtney experimented with each other as innocently as any two young girls at a slumber party might do. Courtney had her first orgasm, and the last one she would have for a long time. She felt closer to Geneva that night than she'd ever felt to anyone before. But the next day, she couldn't look Geneva in the face. Their friendship had been irrevocably changed.

Hurt by Courtney's embarrassment, Geneva began spending time with—of all people—Hank. She soon left altogether, but not before Hank had spent a lot of money on her. It was just another thing Courtney could never forgive him for.

◇

Hank had speed, pot, mushrooms, acid, cocaine. Courtney took

it all, wallowing in the pain of losing Geneva. Not just losing her,

but losing her *to Hank*—what could be more grotesque?

    In addition to the drugs, Courtney started chain-smoking, a

habit that remains with her to this day. She was fifteen, and for

the first time, music that wasn't made by her parents' generation

had begun to carve its way into her consciousness. At reform

school she'd heard protopunk and punk bands such as the

Runaways, the Stooges, the Sex Pistols, the Clash, the Pretend-
ers. "Rock stars" had always seemed as passé to her as tie-dyes
and roach clips. But here was a new kind of rock star, or anti-rock
star. These musicians were a bunch of screaming mutants who
definitely weren't rocking out for world peace. Courtney began to
suspect that there might be a place for her in the glitter-dusted
world of rock.

Her hair was long and feathered, grown out from the first of
many dye jobs to a light golden-brown. She was still flat-chested,
and wore little tank tops and tube tops that accentuated her
prominent nipples. Though she might have been taken for a
groupie, her attitude was pure punk.

Predictably, Courtney and Hank were soon driving each other
crazy. Over and over again throughout his daughter's teens, Hank
would take her in out of guilt, then immediately start nagging her,
cutting her down, telling her she was "fucked up" and "negative."
Courtney, who had inherited his smart mouth, would give it right
back to him. Courtney made plans to return to Portland, where
Linda and her current husband were living. She didn't intend to
live with them, but knew she could crash there if things got dire.
Whether Hank threw her out or she ran away isn't known, but
when Courtney hitchhiked back to Portland, he didn't come looking for her.

Courtney hitchhiked everywhere in those days, and would
continue to do so for several years. She knew that Ted Bundy had
taken victims in and around Portland; she knew about the Green
River Killer, who was going through scads of teenage prostitutes
up north in Seattle, and the I-5 Killer, who trolled highways up
and down the Oregon coast. But she didn't care. And she never
got raped.

Despite her contempt for old-line "rock stars" who came
through town, Courtney went to see Cheap Trick at the Portland
Coliseum. A bunch of girls her age were strutting around in spike

heels and rabbit-fur jackets, their laminated backstage passes dangling conspicuously between their pushed-up breasts. Courtney asked how they got the passes, and the girls laughed at her. Then one of them told her, "You gotta go through the roadie chain. We blow the roadies for these."

Courtney couldn't believe how stupid that was. If you were going to blow the first guy you saw, why bother going backstage at all? Why not just get a pimp? So Courtney—flat-chested Courtney in her baggy jeans and burgundy cashmere sweater—went up to a road manager and simply *talked* two laminates out of him.

It wasn't enough. She saw the show for free, she had drinks backstage, she flirted with Cheap Trick. But when she got back to her stepfather's house, Courtney sat down in one of Linda's antique chairs and cried.

She had watched the band from *backstage,* from their perspective, and it had made her realize that it wasn't the musicians she wanted. She wanted what they felt looking into the audience: the wild churning, the crazed faces, the lighters, the sweat. She wanted their power. She wanted to be playing the music—and the audience.

This desire didn't stop her from talking her way into more bad rock shows; on the contrary, she wanted to learn all she could by watching these privileged few. Soon she had the other groupies vying for her friendship and her spare laminates. Sexually, she didn't go as far with the musicians as the others did; she'd lost her hymen to a speculum at Hillcrest, but she would hang on to her virginity for another year.

Courtney was too envious of the musicians to want to play Lolita for them. Rather, she kept scamming her way backstage hoping that some of that raw power would rub off, that she'd figure out how to make an audience scream and beg for more.

When no bands were in town, she hung out with strippers, punk kids, gay boys, and drag queens. Many of Portland's seamy strip clubs were willing to hire underage punk girls, and Courtney picked up some cash dancing, though she claims to have been "too fat and weird" to make good money. A more likely problem was that she insisted on preserving her artistic integrity by dancing to her favorite music, most of which the customers hated.

Even so, taking off her clothes for money—even the crumpled dollar bills offered up by the sleazy minions of Portland's dives— gave her a taste of the power over an audience that she craved. Perhaps even more important, it occasionally made her feel pretty —an experience she had scarcely known before.

Courtney's haven was the Metropolitan, an all-ages disco where drag queens mothered her and taught her how to be glamorous. These tall, lush, painted hothouse flowers became new role models: better than the bad girls at reform school, better even than the big-haired guitar gods she worshiped now.

She also met acid-tongued scenester Dean Matthiesen, who until late 1996 ran her household in Seattle. Dean's theater troupe, the Bad Actors, often performed at the Met. Once Courtney volunteered to assist in a performance without knowing what was going to happen. Dean tied her up, blindfolded her, and beat her with a frozen fish while singing "The Man Who Got Away."

At this time, Courtney was assigned a new social worker who actually bothered to read her thick file. Seeing that there was a bit of family money available, the woman recommended that her young charge be granted legal and financial emancipation from her parents. The court set up a trust fund that allowed Courtney about five hundred dollars each month. With that and her stripping income, she was able to rent an apartment in northwest Portland.

Courtney's best friends were Ursula Wehr and Robin Barbur, two beautiful girls who were major figures in the Portland punk scene circa 1981. Ursula worked at the Met and called herself Queen of the Fags. Robin had a beautiful singing voice. The three of them decided to start a band, Sugar Babylon, whose practice sessions mostly consisted of drinking coffee at Denny's and talking about the mansions, clothes, and private jets they were going to have when they reached the top of the charts.

They dyed their hair blue-black and teased it high, wore smudged jet-black eyeliner and blood-red lipstick, draped themselves in diaphanous thrift-store finery and far too many bracelets. "It was more like we were *maybe going to be* a band," recalls Ursula, who now sings in the Portland band Candy 500. "We'd get together and drink a lot of wine."

Robin Bradbury (née Barbur) remembers accompanying Courtney to visit Hank in San Francisco. "He took us to see Janis Joplin's old backing band," she recalls, "and then he gave us this Baggie full of microdot. 'Here you go, maybe you girls can take this home and sell it to your friends.' Gee, thanks, Mr. Harrison."

Around the same time, Robin remembers Frank Rodriguez giving his stepdaughter a toothbrush. "I don't think she got the normal things that kids get from their parents. I mean, to get so excited about a fucking toothbrush. Because Frank actually cared about her dental health, and bought this toothbrush for her, that meant more than"—Robin shrugs—"microdot."

Ursula Wehr adds, "Every time Courtney came into some money, she'd buy her mother Joy perfume, all these expensive presents, and she'd come back all depressed because nobody appreciated it enough."

Then "Roger" appeared on the scene and offered Courtney the chance of a lifetime. He chatted up kids in coffee shops, in clubs, on the street. He was an agent of sorts, he said, a man who could help her travel the world and make a lot of money. Roger's deal was sending underage girls to Japan to work in the strip clubs. His Japanese connections—the powerful criminal organization known as the Yakuza—would pay the girl's fare and put her up once she got there.

Courtney already knew how to strip for money, and she leapt at a chance to get out of the country without involving either of her parents. Since she already had a passport, things moved quickly for her, and soon she was on a plane to Japan.

The expensively dressed Japanese man who met her at the airport was missing a pinkie finger (the Yakuza have a custom of severing finger joints to placate superiors they have displeased). He confiscated her passport and drove her in a gleaming little car to the strip club outside Tokyo where she was to work.

Courtney had never seen a setup like this before. All the dancers slept on futons in a single large dressing room where mosquito coils were always kept burning. They were minimally cared for by a mama-san and a papa-san who served them two meals of rice and fish each day. The Brazilian girl from whom Courtney inherited her futon had left behind a batch of crab lice, and Courtney caught them. The whole scene didn't faze her at first; it was like being on Mars. She thought of herself as a neutral observer, an eye that had seen too much. But it was nothing she couldn't handle for $2,500 a week.

She worked the day shift at the club and took the bullet train into Tokyo to get drunk every night. The bars were full of Japanese businessmen who made her slobbering, incomprehensible propositions. At the beginning of Courtney's second month in Japan, the club offered her a raise. It took her a couple of days to figure out that they wanted her to give sexual favors for the additional money. "I didn't realize the fact that I was flat-chested and a virgin made me more valuable to the Yakuza," she would admit years later.

Courtney wasn't ready to sell herself to some Yakuza thug or sadistic salaryman. Since her passport was confiscated, she turned herself in to the U.S. Embassy, which began deportation proceedings. In the meantime, she was kept in a cell with four other women, a Filipino and three Koreans who kept touching her pale skin and hair, and saying *gaijin, gaijin.* Their fingers were gentle, but after four days the constant tugging and ogling felt like slow torture.

Courtney spent the whole time expecting men with three-piece suits and missing fingers to show up and drag her away. She amused herself by wondering whether they would force her into the white-slave trade after all, or just chop her up and throw her in a Dumpster somewhere. But at last they put her on a plane back to Portland. The episode was worth months of bragging rights at the Met.

Soon after returning to Portland, Courtney shook off the last remnants of her rock groupie phase. It was time to get moving. She bought a SID LIVES button, shaved her head, and bought a guitar. She was sick of other people deciding how she should look, how she should act. She was living independently, learning to play her guitar. She knew her way around the scene. To all appearances, Courtney had it made in Portland.

So, perversely, she decided to leave the country again.

◇

This time she went jetting off to Ireland, where she had received

an invitation to visit Hank. Hank claimed that he was teaching a

course at Trinity College in Dublin. (Grateful Dead 101?) It

turned out to be a lie, of course. He wasn't even living in Dublin

proper, but in a drafty old manor house way out in the boondocks

of County Meath.

Courtney didn't want to see BioDad, but with a little trust-

fund money in her pocket, she'd been unable to resist the chance to get out of the country and explore the Celtic roots she'd always suspected she had. Soon, though, she wished she hadn't come.

The night before she left, Hank took her on a pilgrimage to some standing stones in the countryside. "I slept under an Irish moon," she later said, "between Knowth and Dowth, with wild cygnets screaming in the Slaney River nearby, stars in the stones, and all that."

Then she went to Dublin and immediately set about insinuating herself into the music scene. She quickly discovered that English musicians like hanging out in Dublin because Dubliners consider it uncool to let on if they recognize anyone famous. Courtney says she audited a semester and a half of classes at Trinity and became a photographer for Dublin's top music paper, *Hot Press*.

Hot Press has officially denied that Courtney ever worked for them, but a source close to the paper says that their employment records are mysteriously incomplete for this time period. It is easy to imagine the trendy Irish paper hiring this brash young American who claimed to be a guitarist; then again, it's not too hard to imagine Courtney going around town with a camera, talking her way into shows by saying she worked for *Hot Press*.

Whether she was with a magazine or not, she somehow managed to hook up with Julian Cope of The Teardrop Explodes. In her eyes, Cope would quickly become her portal to the tawdry rock magic she craved.

The Teardrop Explodes was a lush dark-pop ensemble. Julian's deep vocals were tremulous with angst. He was thin and lank-haired and golden-eyed. Courtney was enchanted. She snagged the singer's attention by way of a roadie. Julian seemed taken with her immediately. "Do you know Lydia Lunch?" he asked her.

"No, why?"

"Because you're her fucking doppelgänger."

"I am not."

Julian invited her to take acid with him. Courtney said no. He asked why not. She said, "Because I'll get jealous because you're a famous rock star and I'm not."

Julian laughed and laughed. Then, incredibly, he presented her with the keys to his house in Liverpool. "I want you to live with me," he told her.

"You're joking," Courtney said. But she tucked the keys in her bag before he could change his mind.

Soon afterward, Courtney left Dublin for London. There she rented a flat, practiced her guitar, wrote a lot of lyrics, bought a lot of clothes, and wired money to Robin Barbur for a plane ticket, telling the administrators of her trust fund that the money was for "tuition." Robin soon arrived, and the pair spent a few exciting weeks in London before working up the nerve to descend upon Liverpool and see if Julian's offer of lodging had been genuine.

The English music scene circa 1982 was dominated by late punk, early goth, and the burgeoning New Romantic movement. With an emphasis on synthesizers, fantasy makeup, and baroque fashion, New Romantic bands included Soft Cell, Duran Duran, the Human League, and Culture Club as well as The Teardrop Explodes and their mates, Echo and the Bunnymen. (Julian Cope had played with Echo front man Ian McCulloch in the Liverpool punk band the Crucial Three, then kicked McCulloch out of an early version of The Teardrop Explodes.)

They went shopping for clothes when they had money. Otherwise, they talked their way into clubs, shoplifted makeup and cigarettes, and prowled the streets of London with their Walkman headphones on, imagining they were in a video. Robin later said of Courtney in London, "She'd steal your shit, she'd expect you to steal her shit. She'd have no concept of money. We took all the money at the first of the month and bought a dress and a camera and a bottle of Grand Marnier, and then we would starve." During one of the starving periods, they finally sold Hank's Baggie of microdot for ten pounds to buy food, then hitchhiked to Liverpool.

When they found Julian's house, Julian wasn't there, and his housemates were naturally suspicious of these loud American beauties who showed up with numerous suitcases and a key to their home. "Julian said we could stay here," Courtney insisted.

"I wish Julian had *told* me," said Pete de Freitas, drummer for Echo and the Bunnymen. But, after tracking down Julian by phone and confirming Courtney's story, he let the girls stay. They were alarmingly young and obviously had nowhere else to go, and Julian told him Courtney was a "fucking genius."

Life in Liverpool was a blur of pints, acid, and sulfate speed, dressing up and going out, seeing and being seen. The Teardrop Explodes were at the height of their fame, and the band members would say things like, "You girls don't know the position you're in. Every girl in town would love to be here."

Although they were always taken for tourists, they would lie and say Robin's mother was from Liverpool. They were mysteriously hated by Pete Burns, later of Dead or Alive, who worked at the hippest record store in town and had the habit of standing outside its door in a fur diaper and vest verbally abusing people. He dubbed Courtney and Robin "The Ugly Americans," and they called him, variously, "Sir Rooster," "Chicken Little," and "Cunty Assbite."

One day the girls arrived at a friend's wedding reception carrying potted plants as gifts. Pete was there and began loudly claiming that "The Ugly Americans" were unwelcome at the reception. Courtney was so angry that she dropped her plant, which had cost her a lot of money, and punched him.

She made lengthy, detailed lists in her notebooks, an obsessive lifelong practice for her. A list of things she loved while in Liverpool included *Star Trek,* A. A. Milne, Oregon beaches, cherry blossoms, Halloween, Baudelaire, and "The Dance of the Sugarplum Fairies." On her hate list were Pete Burns, Jim Morrison, Quaaludes with lager, Desmond Morris, John Donne, Gurdjieff, black pudding, and the William S. Burroughs method of writing lyrics.

Courtney still listened to punk, goth, and other English music of the day, but she had also developed an appreciation for American singer-songwriters like Tom Waits, Bob Dylan, Lou Reed, and Patti Smith, as well as the Canadian Leonard Cohen. She loved the noise and attitude of punk, but she was also addicted to the lure of a pretty pop song. Her favorite Stone was Keith, but her favorite Beatle was Paul.

She and Robin tried to revive Sugar Babylon. Courtney recruited a bass player, Chrissie, and a drummer, Paul Edward. Robin recalls, "Dave Balfe [keyboard player for The Teardrop Explodes] loaned us a sixteen-track, and of course we didn't have a clue what to do with it, so it sat there and we got nervous about spilling things around it. We didn't know what we were doing. We never played out."

Even if they had, their efforts would have been lost in the glamorous swirl of life with The Teardrop Explodes. The band was at the height of its fame. Julian couldn't go to a club without being mobbed, and Courtney loved being in the middle of it all. But Julian's fame only made Courtney want hers all the more. When her monthly trust-fund payment wouldn't stretch to cover expenses, Courtney wrote to Linda, claiming she planned to go to college in Liverpool and needed more money. The letter ended, "The band I'm in has an imminent recording deal so maybe I'll be so rich you won't have to even bother—Love Courtney."

Julian Cope had an enormous personal influence on Courtney. He was one of the first people to make her feel smart, and he urged her to assert her dormant ego. "Julian told us to live your life as if you're being followed by a movie camera," says Robin

Bradbury. "I remember she started walking very self-assuredly, head up, fast. She really looked up to Julian."

A cute Teardrop groupie who lived across the street, Michael Mooney, was slight and fair, a Pisces who Courtney claims gave her a lifelong taste for the sign. Both of them were in love with Julian, but they settled for consummating it with each other as Joy Division's "Isolation" played in the background. "After we'd done it," Courtney later told *Melody Maker,* "I went across the road for cigarettes and I had all this blood and fluid running down my legs." Michael Mooney has denied that the encounter ever took place.

Pete de Freitas finally evicted the houseguests by leaving them a note. Courtney plotted ways to escape her situation. She could return to Japan to strip. Getting away from the Liverpool scene would show everyone how much they missed her. She'd save enough money to buy the musical equipment she needed. And she would be homesick, and when she got back, everything wouldn't feel so stale and hopeless anymore. Summer was coming, and she tried to convince herself that she missed Tokyo: the bullet trains, the noodle shops, the transition from hot, sticky streets to air-conditioned palaces of commerce.

While Courtney was planning her escape, Robin went out and found a cheap bed-sit, which convinced Courtney to stay in Liverpool a little longer. "The landlord had rented to the Beatles," Robin recalls, "so we were impressed, and of course it was a shithole."

A few weeks after moving in, Courtney wrote,

> I haven't entered into a description of Bedsit because it would be painful. Picture plastic chairs, a view of the garbage, broken fridge/lights/doorbell, prison door, broken window, and lower-class swirlfudgesludgepatterned earth-toned carpet lining up smartly with

sheetless mattress (that I've had a weird time on), textured tawny-beige-green and brown-silver and white-
old-human wallpaper. Plague-colored kitchen (like
walking into a smoker's lung). And the inevitable For-
mica fire. Sumptuous.

The Liverpudlian adventure would continue only a little
longer.

Courtney had a wildly romantic dream about Bernie Albrecht,
the guitarist for New Order, despite the fact that she'd never met
him or even seen a picture. She wrote him a letter about the
dream, invited him to her seventeenth birthday party, and ended
with the line, "I'm disdainful and horrible but if you tell me who
you are I'll melt." Like many of Courtney's missives, it was never
sent.

She put him on one of her want lists, along with a gray Heidi
dress, black lace-up slippers, a cheap romance novel, rehearsal
time, a photo album, a new diary, and (pre-ironically) "a Navy
peacoat, flannel shirt, blue work shirt, and pants patches."

On July 21, just after her birthday, Courtney's visa expired.
She was surprised to realize she didn't care. Her "home" was more
depressing than any correctional institution she'd ever lived in.
She and Robin were sick of each other after six months of living
in absolute proximity (during a recent argument, Courtney had
thrown a pen at Robin and nearly hit her in the eye, which
frightened them both). Her band in its present incarnation was a
joke. She booked a flight back to Portland, leaving Robin to find
her own way home.

Robin's mother hocked her wedding ring for the price of a
plane ticket. Robin actually arrived home before Courtney, safe
but exhausted. She crawled into her bed and slept for nearly
twenty-four hours, then woke, dressed in some of her new English clothes, and went downtown to see Ursula. When Robin

got back home, her mother met her at the door and said, "I don't want you to be upset, but Courtney's here. She didn't have anyone else to pick her up at the airport."

Robin found Courtney in her bed. Half-eaten bagels, magazines, and cigarette butts were everywhere. Anyone else might have been contrite, but Courtney only shoved a peroxided snarl of hair out of her eyes, peered up at Robin, and growled, "Don't give me that look, Barbur. I'll kick your ass."

◇

Compared to England, the Pacific Northwest seemed dreary and

dull. One of Courtney's few joys was showing off the clothes and

records she had acquired overseas, items that wouldn't be available

in the States for another year or more. She slouched around

Portland in an old trenchcoat of Julian's and comforted herself

with the few, widely scattered cool things she was able to find in

America: thrift shops, Iggy Pop records, the embryonic *Sub Pop*

zine published by Bruce Pavitt out of Olympia, Washington.

Soon after her return to the States, Courtney started looking for Geneva. She'd been thinking about her old friend ever since she had seen Hank: wondering where Geneva had fled to, what wild dreams sustained her now. At last she got a lead, an address.

But her hopes were crushed when she found Geneva married to a toothless acidhead, pregnant, getting free food from the Salvation Army, her big beautiful eyes full of lunacy and defeat. Courtney begged Geneva to run away with her, promised to support Geneva and the baby with her trust-fund money, promised that they would start a band together, all but promised to marry her. But Geneva wouldn't go, and finally Courtney walked away alone.

(Years later, Courtney would hire a private detective in an attempt to locate Geneva once more. His efforts were unsuccessful.)

Dean Matthiesen, now managing the Met, was happy to hire Courtney as his DJ. Fresh from six months in England, she had the trace of a scouse accent and an encyclopedic knowledge of new music. She knew the vagaries of the Portland scene. And she was a good sport: she didn't even hold the frozen-fish flogging against him.

Though Courtney would soon move in with Dean and some of the other Bad Actors, she stayed briefly at the Napalm Beach house. Napalm Beach was a popular local band whose communal home, in the tradition of band houses since time immemorial, was a hollowed-out shell of a structure decorated with bare mattresses, graffiti, show fliers, and trash. The band's front man, Chris Newman, was 450 sweaty pounds of guitar god. Courtney still couldn't play guitar very well, but she desperately wanted to. When her trust officer gave her a Christmas bonus, she bought a P.A. She studied Chris's every move onstage and in practice. What she didn't realize at the time was that Napalm Beach were doing their best to sound just like the Stooges.

Newman seemed an odd influence. But Courtney could do

worse, and she was soon to prove it. Since being rejected by her parents, Courtney hadn't let anyone really get to her, really hurt her. She'd loved Geneva and Julian dearly, but she hadn't let them touch the real skin of her soul. Now she was about to offer it up to someone who would happily rip it wide open.

Rozz Rezabek-Wright was a glam-rock fantasy or nightmare, depending on your perspective: sunken-eyed avian features smudged with last night's makeup, thin limbs wrapped in spandex, long neck swathed in chains, pinky-orange hair cut and teased in a style perhaps meant to recall Ziggy Stardust or Sid Vicious, but irretrievably veering more toward Rod Stewart. He sang for Theatre of Sheep, a wispy New Romantic synth-pop ensemble whose logo was a champagne glass with bubbles spilling over the rim. The band included Rozz's fiancée, Leslie, on keyboards.

Courtney's friends weren't impressed with Rozz. "I think his relationship with her was based on the fact that she had a prescription for Valium and some money," says Robin. But he was the embodiment of Courtney's dreams, a creature woven entirely from the brilliant tapestry of rock'n'roll. She was seventeen; he was about ten years older. She read everything she could get her hands on; he owned thirty-seven books, all of them different editions of *Valley of the Dolls*, Jacqueline Susann's paean to broken dreams and the drugs that will make them go away. Rozz had a serious pill fetish, according to Robin: "He was always wasted, he was always on something. I wonder if he made up so much shit about Courtney because he can't remember what really happened."

(Rozz has certainly made some surprising allegations about Courtney in recent years: for example, he says that lyrics he wrote later appeared on Hole's albums, even though he claims not to have heard either of Hole's albums. In 1995 he tried to secure a book deal based on some old journals Courtney had left in his apartment.)

Rozz insisted that their affair be kept secret (an odd stipulation if it was as platonic as he asserted). He didn't want Leslie to find out, and he made no secret of the fact that he was embarrassed to be seen with Courtney. The insecure seventeen-year-old thought of herself as fat and, if not ugly, then certainly not pretty. Rozz homed in on these feelings and took advantage of them with a predator's expertise. If Courtney showed a spark of pride, he could always remind her that Leslie was anorexic and model-gorgeous.

The first time they had sex, Rozz tied Courtney's hands to her bed frame, stuck two barbiturates in her mouth, and poured Wedding Bells champagne over her. In the morning, he asked her to fix him oatmeal. She took special care with it, putting in currants, nutmeg, cinnamon, and whole cream. Rozz took one look at the bowl and hurled it across the kitchen, where it dripped slowly down the wall. "You stupid bitch! Don't you know that *singers don't eat dairy products?*"

As if she needed an extra dose of angst, she saw *A Streetcar Named Desire* for the first time. "I thought, Is that going to be me? I was terrified." Superficially, it may seem histrionic for a seventeen-year-old girl to see herself in a thirty-year-old dowager. However, it is worth recalling a few things about Blanche DuBois as created by Tennessee Williams and played by Vivien Leigh. She is a frankly bleached blonde. She keeps her accessories in a heart-shaped box. She is crucified for being a whore. Her young husband and only true love, a poet, shot himself in the head. During 1994 and 1995, Courtney Love-Cobain often checked into hotels under the name Blanche DuBois.

She and Robin tried to revive Sugar Babylon again, but they had developed serious musical differences (Robin was going through a Duran Duran phase). Courtney did a stint writing the Portland Scene Report for *Maximumrocknroll,* and through this channel began corresponding with a girl in L.A., Jennifer Finch. Finch would later front the seminal band L7, but at that time she was a rabid fan of the Red Hot Chili Peppers who could be seen dancing ecstatically down front wherever the tattooed thrashpunk band was playing. She invited Courtney to visit her in L.A. and start a band.

Courtney was met at LAX by a bad-ass brunette who looked like somebody she'd want to be in a band with. Instead, all they did was go to rock shows, dance themselves into a frenzy, then try to get backstage. A joke among L.A. bands at the time was that you knew you'd made it when Courtney Love and Jennifer Finch got in the front row and took their shirts off.

Back in Oregon, Courtney briefly attended Portland State University, hoping to major in philosophy. Hank sent her Methedrine to help her get through midterms, and a girl in a punk band who was staying with her suggested that they shoot it.

It was the first time Courtney had injected drugs, and as she describes it, "I thought I saw God. And then the comedown was about the worst experience of my life. Then she got more speed and I found myself hitchhiking to San Francisco with a truck driver named Carolina Dragass."

So much for the midterms. But Courtney left the truck driver behind and met a new boy in San Francisco, one who wasn't engaged and didn't think she was ugly. Jeff Mann was a sweet soul who (initially, at least) built up Courtney's confidence as much as Rozz had torn it down. "It set a pattern for relationships my whole life," she said later, "the good boyfriend versus the evil rock-star boyfriend."

She was still convinced that she loved Rozz, and even sent Theatre of Sheep's demo tape to several of her English connections, none of whom paid it any notice. She didn't always capitulate to Rozz, though. On one occasion they flew to San Francisco together, where Rozz sent Courtney out to appointments with as many doctors as possible. She filled her journal with notes on barbiturate dosages and drafts of convincing speeches she could make to the M.D.s. She also left Rozz alone in the hotel room while she went to see Jeff.

Rozz amused himself by writing a self-pitying letter in her notebook:

> Front desk says it's after 2 AM. I feel like a heel. This was to be a glamourous evening at 181 but in all my elegance I pulled a Neely O'Hara Tuinal curtain call. I guess Club 181 is out. I hope you have a lovely visit w/Jeff. If you want to renew and/or carry on some sort of interludely transient romance don't feel obligated to protect me—lies or alibis. . . . In my present situation I can offer few promises or commitments of you and (regardless of twinges of jealousy) demand nothing of you. . . . Do as you please with no regrets and don't feel obligated to tell me lies or protect me with sentimental verbal meanderings. My love is without those ugly tawdries. I just love you—Rozz.

But back in Portland, on Valentine's Day 1983, Rozz left her all alone. Courtney put on black lingerie and a Theatre of Sheep T-shirt and slashed her wrists with her favorite Wilkinson double-edged stainless-steel razor blades. She was taken to the hospital in an ambulance and briefly put on an IV, but no serious harm was done. She recuperated at stepfather Frank's house, the place she always went to for comfort, drinking brandy, writing lyrics and long letters.

When she returned to the house she was sharing with two other girls, her wrist sutures were still fresh, but her roommates were in no state to notice. One was curled up in the trash room in a pseudocatatonic stupor. The other, an artist, was in the bathroom scraping Courtney's dried blood off the tiles to sprinkle on a sculpture.

Rozz was holed up with Leslie and didn't try to contact Courtney for days. When he finally did, he took her to see a movie, got her drunk, helped himself to her Valiums, and jacked off. While all this was going on, Leslie somehow found out where they were and called, threatening suicide, then begging Courtney to leave her man alone.

She ran up huge phone bills talking to Jeff, knowing that she could have a sensible, stable relationship with him, but was unable to tear completely away from Rozz's dark dazzle. They continued to attempt an open relationship, but during the nights Rozz spent with Leslie while Jeff was far away in San Francisco, Courtney had to admit to herself that sex was more important than she would like it to be.

So important, in fact, that she wasn't playing music, though she went clubbing all the time and listened to everything. Her favorite music of the period (from another list) included Flipper, Echo and the Bunnymen, the Runaways, Billie Holiday, Soft Cell, the Dead Kennedys, Lou Reed, Kate Bush, Joni Mitchell, Frank Sinatra, and the Bay City Rollers; her least favorites were the Birthday Party, Henry Mancini, the *Valley of the Dolls* soundtrack, and New Order. She wrote lyrics and poems constantly, but her guitar was gathering dust.

She maintained her longtime therapy habit, cadging dozens of prescriptions, most of which were consumed by Rozz. When she asked her various doctors for an actual diagnosis of her condition, one told her, "Your dramatics turn into histrionics, and you have a compulsive hunger, a need to devour." Another said she was "a mass of unstrung cells trying to form the usual teen-queen identity crisis."

Rozz tantalized her with the bizarre logic that, given some time alone with Leslie, he might break off their engagement. "Why don't you skip town for a little while?" he persuaded Courtney. "Go somewhere and strip. You can send money back to me and I'll put it in a bank account for you."

It is difficult to imagine even an eighteen-year-old buying this line, but Courtney started making plans to go to Taiwan.

CHAPTER SIX

◇

Taiwan was hot, crowded, rickety, and utterly exotic. Courtney

shopped the street markets, lived on fresh fruit and sushi, and

danced at night using the name "Crystal." She wore frosted

eye shadow, feathers and rhinestones, little baby-doll outfits

in pastel colors. And Asian men didn't care if she was a bit

plump.

She had her own hotel room with all the comforts of budget

Asia—a rusty sink, a mosquito coil, even a rabbit-eared television. The high-pitched coos and shrieks of Asian TV were immediately evocative of her Japanese trip two years before.

She wrote to Michael Mooney and looked into the cost of flying him from Liverpool to Taiwan for a visit, but he never came. Sporadically, she missed Jeff and/or Rozz and obsessed about startng a band. She even considered flying Rozz to Tokyo and meeting him there for a vacation, but these limp fantasies paled in comparison to her Technicolor dreams of leadng a rock band.

Instead, Courtney fled to Hong Kong. It was the strangest place she'd ever been, the streets claustrophobically narrow and packed with teetering ramshackle buildings, laundry flapping like prayer flags overhead, the air full of strange, savory smells. All the strippers did heroin, and the fashions seemed perpetually stuck in the seventies. It was a bit like meeting a bunch of Asian Marcia Bradys on junk. Courtney's tiny, windowless hotel room contained a round bed with polka-dot sheets and a beanbag chair.

She got a job at a dime-a-dance place where the girls were required to surrender their passports to the management. When she walked into the back room on her first night, she found a gaggle of young Asian women playing cards and nodding out. One of them directed her to an old petroleum barrel full of evening gowns. All the dresses were too short for Courtney, but she eventually settled on a white satin halter-top number with a rhinestone star on the left breast.

In the course of the evening, Courtney danced with a greasy-haired, potbellied Filipino shipping tycoon who began talking loudly about wanting to do cocaine. Another dancer volunteered to go get some. She left, and the tycoon kept tipping Courtney hugely every fifteen minutes just to stay at his table. *If I stick with this one until four in the morning,* she thought, *I can make half my plane fare home.*

The dancer came back and threw a packet of white powder

on the table. The tycoon immediately started cutting lines. Courtney had never done coke and thought she'd snort a little. It turned out to be pure China White heroin.

She'd been around heroin in San Francisco, but thought it was for idiots. Now she found herself in a stupor of bliss, not caring when the tycoon carried her out of the club and transported her to his hotel suite, where she passed out.

When she woke up hours later, the tycoon took her shopping and bought her a fur coat, then asked her to come back to the Philippines with him. Playing her cards very carefully, Courtney said okay. Delighted, he gave her $10,000 in cash and told her to go buy herself some clothes for the trip.

And so it was that Love Courtney Michelle Harrison Rodriguez Menely found herself at Chiang Kai-shek International Airport with nothing but a white satin halter dress, a fur, and ten grand. She was able to talk her way onto a plane by claiming her passport had been stolen. As she settled back in her first-class seat with a glass of wine, something made her remember the first time she'd met Julian.

You know, she thought with some satisfaction, *I bet Lydia Lunch never did anything like* this.

Back in Portland, she took up with the old crowd again. Rozz dropped out of sight, but refused to say why. Courtney retreated to Frank, who took her to a hippie festival where she had her tarot cards read. The tarot lady's eyes widened in alarm. "Get the hell out of wherever you are," she told Courtney. "Get out and go to school. Don't get pregnant. Someone is sucking you dry and he will not stop, ever, and you won't get to die."

Determined to orchestrate crisis after crisis, Rozz took half a gram of meth and twenty-six Valiums, then disappeared into the streets of Portland. He was a junkie for tragedy, as long as it centered around him. Courtney went out looking for him, exhausted herself walking, finally sat slouched in a doorway as rain began to fall. Voices echoed in her head. Rozz: *I'm terrified of you.*

I don't get a chance to miss you. Robin and Ursula: *He's an asshole, Courtney. You're gonna regret this one.* Frank: *Your youth is slipping away while you kowtow to this guy.* And the fortune-teller: *He's the devil, he's a vampire. Get the hell away from him.*

While Rozz was gone, Courtney went to his apartment, smashed a few things, kicked out a few windows, gathered up all the letters she could find, and left—forever, she hoped.

She lived with Jeff for a while in San Francisco, getting food stamps, taking drugs, and going to punk shows. One night she and her friend Joe Mama drove up to Portland to collect some of her things. Theatre of Sheep was playing a gig. Courtney stormed the stage in stiletto heels and a vintage black lace catsuit (Rozz claims she was wearing a white wedding dress) and tossed several handfuls of empty Valium bottles at Rozz's feet.

Courtney traveled overseas again in 1984, this time to visit Liverpool and, she hoped, to see some of Europe. She caught up with the old crowd and made some new friends, heroin users among them. One day she went to a council flat in Liverpool to score two grams. The skaghead who lived there was already smoking it when Courtney arrived, and the smell made her nauseous. She smoked some anyway, got incredibly high, and was suddenly amazed to realize that she didn't care about men at all. Relationships got in the way of ambition, she decided, and she couldn't afford to have one. Michael Mooney, now on tour with the Psychedelic Furs, disapproved of her drug use. Fuck him! Fuck them all! She didn't need them! Now if only she could hang on to that conviction once she got back to the States.

When she finally ran into Julian one rainy afternoon, she received a heartbreaking snub from him. He pretended not to see her, and when she confronted him, he told her, "I've got nothing to say to you. I have tunnel vision at the moment." Courtney felt she'd worn out her second welcome in Liverpool, so she scraped together the last of her money and went to Paris. But though she loved the gilded decay of Paris itself, the thousands of sylphlike fashion goddesses strolling through its streets only made her feel frumpier than ever. It was time to go home.

On her last night in Paris, she glued a postcard of decadent poet Arthur Rimbaud in her notebook, bathed in the light of a full moon, and contemplated dyeing her hair green (deciding against it because she knew she'd have to get a job soon). "I am born first of purity, and secondly and most important of desperation," she wrote.

Upon her return to the States, she halfheartedly resumed shuttling between hapless, monstrous Rozz and tender, passive Jeff but soon lost interest. She began to focus her energy on her own work and on the dream of starting a band rather than frittering her intensity away by juggling losers.

Rozz was as nasty as ever, and Jeff was looking worse and worse. No longer the nice boyfriend, he asked Courtney to move to L.A. with him and get a "real job." He discouraged her musical ambitions and tried to convince her that making it as a musician was no more likely than winning the lottery. Initially, Jeff had endured the presence of Rozz without much complaint, but now he retaliated by starting an affair with one of Courtney's girlfriends.

At least temporarily, her travels had robbed her of her taste for drugs. She believed that the process of giving up drugs was making her even less attractive—and we can be sure Rozz did nothing to dispel this conviction—but she decided to use her self-imposed period of ugliness and anonymity to cultivate her tastes and harden her emotions. She had nothing to lose, and everything to gain.

The Psychedelic Furs were touring the U.S. with a hit single, "Pretty in Pink," which later inspired the John Hughes movie of the same name. Courtney sent her old crush Michael Mooney a dozen long-stemmed white roses in De Kalb, Illinois. Hearing that he had been delighted by the gesture, she decided it would be nice to see him again. When the band played Los Angeles, though, she flew down in a beaded dress that had once belonged to Frances Farmer—and, crushingly, was refused backstage access because the Bangles were visiting the band.

Michael later met her for tea and apologized. For Christmas that year, she sent him a pearl in sandalwood oil.

Courtney was now stripping in San Francisco clubs, and the work seemed grubbier and more depressing than ever. The longer you work as a stripper, the sloppier you get with the makeup, the shaving, the attitude. You stop bothering to repair little flaws in your costumes. You become a lazy cynic whose entire aspect screams, "Just give me a goddamn dollar and leave me the fuck alone." Only the fact that she now condescended to dance to sleazy rock hits instead of esoteric glam-punk allowed her to make any money at all.

One night as she was leaving Rozz's place to look for drugs, she ran into an old acquaintance. Clay was a transplanted New Yorker who had become a guerrilla graffiti artist, scrawling and spray-painting SEX IS REVENGE all over San Francisco. He was inscribing this phrase on the back of Rozz's building.

A few weeks later someone countered Clay's scrawls with their own phrase, LOVE IS REVENGE. Courtney couldn't resist. She went all around town with a marker and spray paint, writing her own name above this so that it read, COURTNEY LOVE IS REVENGE.

Depressing news came from England: Julian Cope was planning to give up the music business, marry a novelist called Dorian, and move to Hawaii. Courtney was momentarily heartbroken. He'd forgotten her. But her fantasies cheered her: someday when she was famous, she'd flare up into his life again, waving a big gold and pink flag, smiling and throwing posies at him. "C'mon," she'd say, "you lost your fame—you lost your marbles— but you ain't lost me."

For now, she dismissed Julian and Dorian as "selfish, pomp-ous, and lardy." Then she wrote out a template for a new band:

> Form by end of January 1985
> Gig Feb—March
> Record by April
> Wembley Oct 85

◇

Faith No More was founded in 1982 by San Francisco drummer

Mike Bordin, with L.A. transplants Billy Gould and Roddy Bot-

tum on bass and keyboards. The trio poached a guitarist, Jim

Martin, from a local thrash band. They had a revolving series of

singers—one of whom, for an undetermined and hotly disputed

period of time, was Courtney Love, who initially became a fan of

the band because they reminded her of Killing Joke. Tired of the

postpunk same-sounding bands she had been listening to,

Courtney wanted to find a group with a more melodic sound and more dramatic, profound aspirations. She found that in Faith No More.

On at least one occasion, members of Faith No More have acknowledged that Courtney was in the band, but commented, "Courtney's not the sort of person you can be equal with in a band. She's got to lead and tell people what's what. She was a dictator and in our band things were democratic, so she had to be told to fuck off."

Plausible enough, except possibly the last bit—harmonious band democracies being about as common as functional communist governments. But in other versions of their history, Faith No More denies that Courtney was ever in the band except as an occasional volunteer singer from a club audience. A review in a local magazine, which found the band "unremarkable except for the lead singer," may have rankled.

By her own account, Courtney sang with Faith No More for almost a year after meeting Roddy Bottum at a Lydia Lunch show. As a "hardcore death rock" band, they opened for gory, noise-oriented acts like Specimen, Alien Sex Fiend, and the Butthole Surfers. During one show Courtney smashed a bottle, rolled around in the broken glass, and set her hair on fire—a tribute to one of her heroes, Iggy Pop.

Whatever they considered the extent of her contribution—a slight increase in attendance at their live performances and an injection of pop sensibility into their songs—the other members of Faith No More kicked Courtney out of the band sometime in 1985. She was upset, but upon her return to Portland, she met the person who was to be one of the most important musical influences of her life.

Kat Bjelland's mother had left the family when she was five, and Kat was raised by a mostly absent father. Though she spent her teenage years on the cheerleading squad and the basketball team instead of in juvenile halls and strip clubs, she would come home after school and "sit in this big overstuffed chair and listen to Billie Holiday, read Sylvia Plath, drink Kahlúa from my dad's liquor cabinet, and fantasize how I was going to get the fuck out of here."

She tended to play the part of the cute bratty girl, making big innocent eyes and uttering drop-dead cynical gems in a teeny little voice. It was an image she would later hone and cultivate professionally, which would lead to conflict with Courtney. But in 1985 they hit it off.

Kat was dating a member of the Miracle Workers, a sort of punk sixties-throwback band. Courtney was friends with the singer. The two girls met in a café and discovered that they were both strippers who wanted to be in bands. Courtney thought Kat was funny, sexy, and tough. They went to Kat's place, took Valium and drank wine, talked and listened to Leonard Cohen. "She tried to wash my face for me," Kat recalls, "because I have this really bad habit of drinking and going to sleep with my makeup on, so I learned how to take care of my skin from her . . . When I met her she was really cool and energetic and vibrant and we were really close from then on. It was like finding a soul mate, a sister-type person."

Kat played guitar, and she practiced with Courtney and Robin a few times, but there was no chemistry between the three. Robin thought Kat was snotty, and Courtney decided Robin had "intense L.A. damage." Finally Robin told Courtney to choose between her and Kat. "Robin was wearing a Hard Rock Cafe T-shirt at the time," Courtney said later, "so I chose Kat."

As befitted a person put into therapy as a toddler, Courtney was always on the lookout for a magical remedy to cure some or all of her problems, and she took up a regimen of exotic stress treatments whenever she could afford them. Her favorites included acupuncture, astrology (which she still practices), and the

Bach flower remedies, a complex system of mysticism, homeopathy, and aromatherapy. Disturbed by the cravings she got for pills and, less often, heroin, she also began sporadically attending Narcotics Anonymous meetings. She hoped these pursuits would help her to control her dependence on men, to focus more sharply on her own fame.

She dreamed that Pete de Freitas from the Bunnymen showed up at her place unexpectedly. In the dream, Courtney was fatter than she'd ever been in real life and too strung out on downers to greet him. The apartment reeked of cat piss and squalor, and Pete stared at her with naked disdain.

She decided it was time to get out of Portland. She and Kat made an experimental trip to Seattle, where they stayed with rock promoter Susan Silver, who would later manage Soundgarden and marry lead singer Chris Cornell. "We only saw three cute guys in the whole town," Courtney complained.

Years before the grunge explosion, heroin was already rampant in Seattle. Kat wanted to try it and begged Courtney to get her some. Courtney gave her codeine cough syrup instead. She liked doing junk, but she didn't want to live in a junkie town.

Theatre of Sheep had just broken up, and Rozz had moved to San Francisco. Maybe Courtney still held out hope for him, or maybe she was just sick of Portland and nostalgic for her hometown. At any rate, she quickly made arrangements to return to San Francisco, taking Kat with her in order to finally start a band. They moved into a spacious, high-ceilinged apartment and decorated it with the torn lace, dried roses, candles, and antique baby dolls they both adored.

In Los Angeles, Jennifer Finch had just auditioned on bass for the Pandoras, who said she wasn't cool-looking enough to join their proto-Grrrl band. When Courtney called her, Jennifer was thrilled to join her friend in San Francisco. They rented a big house on Fillmore Street, did drugs, went to shows, argued the merits of Sylvia Plath versus Anne Sexton, found joy in Fleetwood Mac's *Rumours*, wore out copies of *Sgt. Pepper's*, and window-shopped for guitars. When they saw Frightwig, one of the harshest female bands ever, they knew they had to get their own band started.

In June 1985, Courtney Love, Kat Bjelland, and Jennifer Finch formed Sugar Baby Doll (Courtney's improvement on Sugar Babylon). These three women would go on to front three of the most important female-dominated groups of the next decade. Sugar Baby Doll, however, was less than a harbinger of greatness.

"We were going to make the most obnoxious music in the world," Courtney recalls. "However, I had a doctor who gave me a hundred sedatives a week. So we ended up making this sort of faux Cocteau Twins music, but I didn't really have the voice, and I was singing in a register way too high for me."

Courtney still performs one Sugar Baby Doll song, "Best Sunday Dress." A droning melody whose lyrics consist of three lines repeated over and over about dresses and walking into fires, it has an interesting aura of menace, but sounds simplistic next to almost any Hole song.

She saw Jeff Mann around town, on buses and at shows, but he avoided her. He had had enough rivals, enough suicide attempts, enough of Courtney's gale force of a personality. And he was deeply involved with someone else.

Of course, two personalities as strong as Kat's and Courtney's were bound to get on each other's nerves. Courtney, so used to making her own way in the world, thought Kat was terribly spoiled. She couldn't help that she was petite and Dresden-doll pretty, but she was also a prima donna to the core. She quit her job and refused to call her father for money, so most of their expenses fell to Courtney.

But Kat was a good guitarist, and that made it all worthwhile

—until, at a practice session after their third gig, Kat kicked Courtney out of the band. Sugar Baby Doll quickly dissolved, though the trio kept living together because none of them could afford to move.

During that summer, Courtney made a list of the different drugs she had taken during her life. The list began with the LSD she had been given at the age of four and included all the major narcotic groups and several basic stimulants as well as red meat, squatting, ugly boys, and a mixture of baby laxative, Folger's coffee, chocolate pudding, and dirt.

In the same journal, Courtney wrote notes to a hypothetical child that read more like notes to herself—though she did record that her first daughter would probably be named Frances. (Other possibilities included Claire, Willow, and Violet.) Among her bits of advice were, "Opiates and cocaine don't let you get anything done—they're liars"; "Alcohol and cigarettes are weaknesses, disgusting ones; don't have weak flesh"; and "Reading is a really good thing—it's a departure from squalor."

Soon after the band broke up, Jennifer disappeared, leaving a note that read, "I love you, I love Kat, but I love the Chili Peppers more. I'm going home." Courtney couldn't afford to live by herself. She took off to track down Jennifer in L.A.

Jennifer was picking up extra cash playing "punk" characters on TV shows. Courtney got in on the action, appearing in a nightclub scene on the infamous "punk-rock episode" of *Quincy, M.E.* (Plot in a nutshell: When a slam-dancing punk is murdered with an ice pick in the mosh pit, L.A. coroner Quincy takes the music—and the entire punk milieu—to task for "inspiring violence." At the end of the show, we hear Glenn Miller playing in the background as Quincy ruminates, "Why would anyone want to listen to music that makes you hate . . . when you can listen to music that makes you love?")

Work as an extra was unsteady. Courtney soon took a job

dancing at the notorious Jumbo's Clown Room, a pasties-and-G-string joint in a minimall near Hollywood Boulevard. (One of her *Rolling Stone* covers hangs behind the bar at Jumbo's now.)

That was when Nancy entered her life.

◇

In her book *And I Don't Want to Live This Life*, Deborah Spun-

gen describes the behavior of her baby daughter Nancy in terms

eerily similar to those Linda later used to describe Courtney. ("I

cuddled her," Spungen writes of Nancy at six months. "She re-

acted by suddenly stiffening her body like a board, arms and legs

thrust out straight, head thrown back. She screamed even

louder.") Nancy was never diagnosed as autistic, but she spent her

early years in and out of institutions, then found (at least temporary) solace in a burgeoning music scene, just as Courtney would later do.

Nancy Spungen was born on February 27, 1958, cyanotic and jaundiced. She grew up to worship musicians, especially English ones. Rock music and, later, punk were the only comforts she ever found. The love of her life, Sid Vicious, gutted her with a hunting knife in the Chelsea Hotel when she was twenty, then OD'd on heroin.

It was a part Courtney could relate to. She was in love with the myth of the tortured female persona because she thought she could redeem it. She knew she could play it from the moment she first heard about *Sid and Nancy*. The film was to be directed by Alex Cox, who had just made the cult classic *Repo Man*. The open-call audition was announced in *Flipside* and *Maximumrock-nroll*. The turnout consisted of five hundred bleached blondes wearing too much makeup, all of whom had to play a scene where Nancy sees herself in a mirror and shrieks in horror, "*Sid! Help me! I look like fuckin' Stevie Nicks in hippie clothes!*"

Again, Courtney could relate. Out of hundreds of actresses, she was one of a few called back.

When her turn came, Courtney distinguished herself by ripping a picture off the wall and smashing it over Cox's head. He may or may not have been charmed, but he was certainly reminded of Nancy. However, Cox wasn't the only one making the casting decisions. There were still countless callbacks to attend and channels of approval to go through before she would know if she was Nancy.

Life continued apace: a strange man in a restaurant called her by name. When Courtney asked if she knew him, he replied that he'd been on her flight to L.A., where she'd been drunk and staggering the aisles, handing out pills to anyone who had cool hair. She toyed with the idea of suicide again, but abandoned it, feeling that her chances were too obviously great.

She studied *And I Don't Want to Live This Life* and made

notes on Nancy's character. Nancy had to have "That Look," a smoldering glare that usually presaged violence. She had to have big tits (Courtney stuffed her bra for the callbacks) and a New Jersey accent. "Walk around a high school," Courtney instructed herself. "Feel that old degradation. Then go to a rock concert." (Another of her notes reads, "Audition—Make some cookies. Give them in character." One can only imagine.)

Finally the field was narrowed down to three actresses. Courtney's final audition was scheduled. She had recently become interested in Zen Buddhism, and she chanted furiously. Then at last it was done. She had only to wait for the news. She knew she had gotten the part. If by some insane chance she hadn't, she would go off to Guam (which she thought was a foreign country, not a U.S. territory) and be a stripper for the rest of her days.

She didn't get Nancy. Alex Cox still wanted her, but the British producer thought she was too young for the part, and the casting director was disturbed by her lack of experience. The part went to Chloe Webb, who was twenty-eight at the time, and Courtney went to Guam.

There she got a job at Brandy How's strip club near the U.S. Army base. Brandy How was a hard-assed Korean businesswoman who, unbeknownst to Courtney, expected her girls to turn tricks with the soldiers. She also wanted Courtney to change her image with a wig and blue eyeshadow. Courtney wouldn't do any of it, so Brandy How made her dance in the back room instead of on the main stage. Three videos played over and over: a Japanese porn flick, a Korean porn flick, and *Caligula*. To this day, Courtney can recite enormous chunks of the dialogue from *Caligula*.

She spent three weeks at Brandy How's before Alex Cox tracked her down. He had written a small part for her—Gretchen, one of Nancy's American friends. As usual, she had to make a perilous escape, since she was under contract for three months in Guam. She got out of Brandy How's club without being noticed, but by the time she reached the airport, two huge Samoans were on her tail. They chased her through the airport until she ran up to a security guard and screamed, "These men are trying to kidnap me!" The Samoans backed off, and Courtney boarded her flight home.

The parts of *Sid and Nancy* in which Courtney appears were shot in New York City during the winter of 1985. The cast stayed in the Chelsea Hotel on West Twenty-third Street, and several of them ceremonially snorted heroin in Room 101, where Nancy died.

At first it was galling to be on the set with someone else in the role Courtney had obviously been born to play, but she liked Chloe, and she had to admit the more experienced actress was looking good as Nancy. Alex did everything in his power to make things go smoothly for Courtney; he asked her to help cast extras and gave her friend Joe Mama a job in wardrobe. The work paid well, it was more fun than stripping, New York beat the hell out of Guam, and it was a chance to get a foothold in the movie business.

Courtney became convinced that she wanted to be an actress. The demise of Sugar Baby Doll had temporarily soured her enthusiasm for bands.

Sid and Nancy premiered at the 1986 New York Film Festival at Lincoln Center. Courtney appears in four scenes. She helps the lovers score heroin in a blighted tenement; she clutches a kitten in a smoky nightclub; she chatters about her depressed boyfriend; she tearfully insists to the cops that Sid Vicious couldn't have killed Nancy. Her hair is platinum blonde and teased, her face slightly chubby, her eyes huge and blasted-looking and riveting. After the premiere party, Courtney commandeered a limo and made the driver give her a tour of Harlem.

After the movie was finished, Courtney returned to San Francisco. With her own apartment and her *Sid and Nancy* money, she cajoled Kat into reviving the band. This time they called themselves Babes in Toyland. They also decided to move to Minneapolis, a city with an exciting and vital music scene where Hüsker Dü, the Replacements, and Soul Asylum were taking off and where Kat's father now lived, thinking a new home base would reenergize them.

Courtney found the Midwest exotic: "It was so exciting, it was winter, it was like going to Japan, it was grain-belt beer, the CC Club, and all the guys were cute." But her confidence took a plunge when Kat kicked her out of her own band—again. Kat was the one person who knew how much Courtney wanted to be a musician, who shared her raw longing. If Kat still thought she was too awful to play with—well, maybe she didn't have a future in music after all. With that thought, she realized there was absolutely nothing else she wanted to do with her life. She spent a month adrift, working out at the gym, going to Narcotics Anonymous meetings, chanting every day.

At the end of the month she got a call from Alex Cox. He wanted her to come to Spain and star in a movie, and he would pay her $40,000.

◇

Shot in Almería, Spain, *Straight to Hell* was the spaghetti western

to end all spaghetti westerns—quite literally so, for anyone who

saw it as their first example of the genre would never want to see

another. Alex Cox reputedly wrote the script during a three-day

marijuana binge, which is an insult to marijuana. Put simply,

Straight to Hell sucks, it is famous for sucking, and almost every-

one involved with it freely admits that it sucks. But they had a

great time making it.

Courtney plays Velma, a bank robber's moll—or, as she describes the part, "a white-trash pregnant bitch, some weird hillbilly from an incestuous background who's fascinated with charms and magic. She's into tackiness." The only evidence we see of charms and magic is an old cow skull she picks up near the beginning of the movie, but the tackiness is borne out by the polka-dotted maternity dress with black bra showing that she wears through much of the film. She screams most of her lines (she has become a much more powerful screamer since then) and dies in a fiery car crash (one of the few characters who doesn't get shot).

The other stars and cameo players include Joe Strummer of the Clash, Shane MacGowan and Cait O'Riordan of the Pogues, Elvis Costello, Grace Jones (whom Courtney later described to *New Musical Express* as psychotic), director Jim Jarmusch, and real actor Dennis Hopper. The movie has a few funny bits (a town of coffee addicts, a hapless wiener seller, Hopper's cameo), some actual decent acting from Sy Richardson as Courtney's badass boyfriend Norwood, and a couple of rousing musical numbers, but it was not destined to further Courtney's acting career.

Spain reminded her of Taiwan—"suppressed culture, communism, socialism." Surrounded by rock stars, she got a crush on a cameraman. She read Jean Genet even though it made her feel pretentious. Two people asked for her autograph, and Joe Strummer showed her the etiquette of signing one's name for other people: "(1) Gracefully, (2) Dated, (3) Nicely." But she became somewhat disillusioned with Strummer when they were sitting by the hotel pool singing old Clash songs and he forgot the words to "London Calling."

After the movie wrapped, Courtney flew to London. There she renewed contact with Julian Cope (who was at least civil, if not friendly, this time) and received a mysterious invitation from Kat to come back to Minneapolis and rejoin Babes in Toyland.

While contemplating Kat's offer, Courtney lived in the basement of an English rock star, working as a nanny for his children. A close friend of both parties claims that the rocker "used her as a beard. He'd tell his girlfriend, 'I'm just going to have a beer with Courtney,' and he'd leave her sitting on a bar stool by herself for two hours while he went and fucked some girl." She quit the nanny job and went to stay with another well-known rock star and his wife, who kicked her out when she declined to participate in a ménage à trois.

When *Straight to Hell* premiered in London in March 1987, its own cast nearly laughed it off the screen. Courtney and Joe Strummer went out for drinks afterward, and she told him, "I'm gonna move to Minneapolis and start a garage band."

"That's wonderful," he told her, "although you *are* the worst guitarist I've ever heard."

"I don't give a fuck."

The press hated *Straight to Hell* but loved Courtney—they knew a good story when they saw one. She appeared in *People, Us, Film Comment,* and *Interview,* on MTV's *Andy Warhol's 15 Minutes* and *The Cutting Edge.* She and Kat had often used the abbreviation "KWIA," for "Knows Who I Am." Now everyone in London knew who Courtney was.

She fell in love with the press. She had no idea of the long, hard row she had yet to hoe with them. The distance she has since come can be measured by a passage from a letter she wrote to a friend back in the States: "It was awful tonight. Rex Reed called Chloe [Webb] UGLY on national TV!! I am finally completely glad I did not play Nancy Spungen. Oh God I'd die if I got called UGLY on NATIONAL TELEVISION."

She'd been seriously considering Kat's invitation. Finally, now that the premiere was over, she decided to accept it. Joe Strummer gave her the money to fly home.

It soon became obvious that this incarnation of the band, with Michelle Leon on bass and Minneapolis music ambassador Lori Barbero on drums, would be as difficult as all the others. "It's

turned into an exorcism with good products rather than a produc-
tive union," Courtney wrote after only a week.

But Kat was trying. Courtney wrote,

> I'm sure it'll last a month and she'll get bored, but for
> now what a sweety she's being. I guess it's because 80%
> of the boys she likes are super-scared of big loud girls
> with presence and they think girls should be like what
> they think Kat is, which means 80% of her boyfriends
> only like her because she's soft and cute and not be-
> cause she's clever or hard at all, which is why she
> PLOWS through 'em.

She had a rare conversation with her mother. Linda, now into
Buddhist conscious-reincarnation theory, asked Courtney why
she'd chosen her and Hank as parents. Courtney told her, "Because the only parents who could drive someone to celebrity are
ones who aren't there."

Kat holed up for days, decided Courtney was impeding her
progress, and kicked her old friend out of the band yet again. For
the next several days Courtney did nothing but write in her
journal, cut her arm with a razor, and make blood prints on the
pages. She hadn't cut herself for years and years, but the old ritual
was a relief. As always, the physical pain helped drain off some of
the emotional pain.

Courtney then went to New York and made a brief, miserable
attempt to revive her acting career, hanging out with Brat Packers
and reading for movies like *Less Than Zero, Casual Sex?*, and
Earth Girls Are Easy. An agent told her she was a cross between
Madonna and Fanny Brice. She kept getting offered funny-fat-
girl roles instead of the romantic leads she wanted.

Dean Matthiesen and some of the other Bad Actors were in
New York, and one of her few comforts was drinking and doing

Ecstasy with them at East Village dives like the Pyramid Club and ABC No Rio. Sometimes she played parts in their fucked-up theater pieces, but only after making Dean promise that no frozen fish would be involved. She got a starring role in an off-Broadway production called *The Beard*, and things seemed briefly to be looking up. But when the play's run ended, she couldn't find another job.

Unable to deal with life below the poverty line in New York City, Courtney soon returned to Minneapolis. She and Lori Barbero organized a disastrous rock show at the Orpheum. They borrowed thousands of dollars to set up and publicize the event, which featured the Butthole Surfers and several other bands. The show bombed. They found themselves $25,000 in debt, unable to pay the bands, and ostracized by a large portion of the Minneapolis music scene.

She'd been dating a drummer named Dave, whose only redeeming feature was a face as exquisitely beautiful as a Botticelli painting come to life. When Courtney decided to move again—this time back to L.A.—Dave announced that he was going with her. Courtney didn't want him to. The other members of his band hated her for "stealing" him. Her trust fund had finally run out for good, and it was difficult to do the couch tour with a boyfriend who wouldn't get a job, created huge messes wherever he stayed, and didn't understand that it wasn't okay to eat other people's food. At one point he owed her so much money that she threatened to go to work for an escort service unless he sold his stereo and gave her the cash. He told her to go ahead, but she recommenced stripping instead.

One night when Courtney and Dave were visiting, a friend in a local punk band OD'd in her kitchen. Courtney wrote about it to a friend later: "Dave and I CPR'd her navy blue and purple corporeal mortician delite back to life. I met trouble and trouble met me."

Courtney and Dave moved from one sleazy hotel to the next, sometimes going hungry for days. Dave still refused to work. Courtney chanted furiously, but nothing seemed to get better.

In October, Courtney went to Las Vegas hoping to make some quick money stripping, but none of the clubs were hiring when she arrived. When she called home, Jennifer Finch told her that Dave had been sent home to his parents and all his friends in both L.A. and Minneapolis were saying Courtney had driven him crazy.

She finally got work at a club in Vegas. A girl there told her about a supposedly great stripping job in, of all places, Alaska. A club called P.J.'s would fly girls there (sight unseen!) and put them up.

"I decided to move to Alaska because I needed to get my shit together and learn how to work," Courtney said in 1994. "So I went on this sort of vision quest . . . I got rid of all my earthly possessions. I had my bad little strip clothes and some big sweaters, and I moved into a trailer with two other strippers."

One of the strippers had a baby. Courtney loved taking care of the child. She had arrived during the season of twenty-four-hour darkness, and she often saw the fantastic colors of the aurora borealis flickering across the sky. She remained blissfully unaware of a serial killer in the area dismembering numerous female victims, some of whom were strippers. Despite the onus of the job, which turned out not to be as lucrative as she'd hoped, Alaska was a peaceful interlude in her life. For three months she worked, wrote, spoke to almost no one.

And, as always, she listened to music. It was 1988, and interesting things were happening in the Pacific Northwest—not in Portland, where a sort of sixties punk ethic still held sway, but in Seattle. Though it had spawned some good bands, Seattle had never had much of a scene to speak of. Now, apparently, it was the place to be.

Earlier in the eighties, music writer Bruce Pavitt had relocated from Olympia to Seattle, where he parlayed his *Sub Pop* zine into a ground-breaking independent record label. His high school friends from Illinois, Kim Thayil and Hiro Yamamoto, followed him to Seattle and started the band Soundgarden with firebrand singer/drummer Chris Cornell. In 1987 Sub Pop released Soundgarden's debut EP *Screaming Life*, which sparked major-label interest in the "Seattle sound."

Another seminal Seattle band, Green River, split off to form Mother Love Bone and Mudhoney (and, later, Pearl Jam). Skinny blonde Mudhoney front man Mark Arm caught Courtney's attention, as did the sludgy, distorted guitars. Mudhoney's EP *Superfuzz Bigmuff*, also on Sub Pop, would cling to the U.K. indie charts for an entire year. Soon after its release, Sub Pop took a gamble on "Love Buzz," the first single by a band called Nirvana.

Courtney would credit the Mudhoney EP as one of her biggest influences, but she didn't buy "Love Buzz" or anything else Nirvana put out. She'd heard the single, but its pseudo-Eastern sound didn't interest her. Later, back in Portland, she would contemplate buying a Nirvana single at the record store where Dean Matthiesen worked. The problem was, she also wanted the new single by a band called Cat Butt, and she only had enough money for one. She looked at the cover shot of "Kurdt Kobain" with his Harley-Davidson T-shirt and long metal-boy hair, sighed, and chose the Cat Butt single. At least they were comparatively well-dressed.

Third-grade photograph.

Courtney and stepmother Shawn (Frank Rodriguez's ex-wife) blowing bubbles.

Christmas, age eleven.
© Frank Rodriguez

Courtney (far right) and friends at Hillcrest School, 1979.

Gothed out at fifteen.

© Frank Rodriguez

In a crowded photo booth with Robin
Barbur (top right) and at least two
unidentified friends.

Robin Barbur Bradbury

Sugar Babylon (left to right: Courtney,
Ursula Wehr, Robin Barbur).

© Fotografata du Duvall

Taiwan, 1984. Courtney shopped the street markets, lived on fresh fruit and sushi, and danced at night using the name "Crystal."

Courtney in Liverpool. "Julian [Cope] told us to live your life as if you're being followed by a movie camera," Robin Barbur Bradbury remembers.

© *Robin Barbur Bradbury*

Courtney in Alex Cox's western *Straight to Hell*.

Photofest

Courtney with Kurt and his mother, Wendy O'Connor.
Courtney and Wendy are still close.
© Chuck Fradenburg

Kurt, age one, with his parents,
Donald and Wendy Cobain.
© Chuck Fradenburg

Kurt, age two, with Donald.
© Chuck Fradenburg

On February 24, 1992, Kurt and Courtney were married in Waikiki.
Courtney wore a diaphanous white dress that once belonged to Frances Farmer.
Kurt wore blue plaid pajamas, love beads, and a woven Guatemalan purse.
They carried identical pink and white bouquets, but only Kurt was high.

The bride and groom with Nirvana drummer Dave Grohl.

Kurt with Frances Bean.
© Jackie Farry

Kurt's visit with one of his favorite authors, William S. Burroughs, in Lawrence, Kansas, October 1993. After Kurt left, Burroughs said to his secretary, "There's something wrong with that boy. He frowns for no good reason."
© James Grauerholz

Courtney with Frances.
© Jackie Farry

Courtney with Frances, 1993.

© Jackie Farry

Frances with her parents, 1993.

© Jackie Farry

Kurt, Courtney, and Frances at the 1993 MTV Music Awards.
Tammie Arroyo/Celebrity Photo

Frances Bean Cobain's attitude toward the world.
© Jackie Farry

Frances with her father, 1992.
Photo by Guzman

Courtney and Michael Stipe, 1996.
Lisa O'Connor/Celebrity Photo

"Just you try to hold me down /
Come on try to shut me up"
—Courtney Love, "Gutless"

Photo by Ellen von Unwerth

Living through it.
Photo by Andrzej Liguz/Retna

Courtney and Drew Barrymore.
© David Allen/Corbis

An early publicity shot
(left to right: Courtney Love, Jill Emery, Eric Erlandson, Caroline Rue).
Photo by Michael Lavine/Outline

Courtney and Gianni Versace.
© Magnani/Liaison

Courtney and Donatella Versace.
© Magnani/Liaison

At the Film Festival of Berlin for *The People vs. Larry Flynt*, 1997.
From left to right: Edward Norton, Milos Forman, Courtney Love.
R. Siemoneit/Sygma

Photo by Frank W. Ockenfels 3

◇

After three months in the dark, Courtney left Alaska and headed

home by way of Vancouver, British Columbia. She spent a few

weeks in a windowless room in an orange boarding house, still

too fat to get a good stripping job, working on Sundays when the

lithe silicon-breasted blondes took the day off. Soon she jumped

on the Greyhound and got off in Seattle.

"I had little visions of Kurt [Cobain] and Mark [Arm] in my

head," she later told rock writer Pamela Des Barres, "not in a sexual way, but . . . because every town has its sort of rock-star icon guy, the king of the town. And in my head I was like, 'Yeah, when I get my band together, you're going to open for me.' Which is a great way of taking that energy, the sexual energy that comes from rock, and changing it."

But this change was not yet to be wrought. "I walked two blocks away and went to get a room," she recalled. "And in those two blocks I figured out it would take four months before every-one in that city would hate my guts."

Courtney returned to the bus station and managed to convince the clerk that her ticket had been printed wrong and she was really supposed to go to Portland.

Courtney spent two months in Portland trying to get a band together and dating a record-store owner, a beautiful half-Mexican with butternut skin and chocolate eyes who encouraged her interest in new music. One night she went to see the Dharma Bums at Satyricon. The opening act was Nirvana.

Beneath his veneer of stringy blonde hair, snarling vocals, and road-tour grime, the singer was strikingly beautiful—the kind of boy you could hang on a charm bracelet. She wasn't impressed with their set, though, and dismissed them as "love-rockers from Olympia." When Kurt Cobain walked by her table after the show, he glared at her, and Courtney glared back.

He pulled up a chair and poured himself a beer from her pitcher, those achingly blue Charlie Manson eyes still fixed on hers. ("I thought she looked like Nancy Spungen," Kurt later said. "She looked like a classic punk-rock chick. I did feel attracted to her. Probably wanted to fuck her that night, but she left.")

After they exchanged unpleasantries, Kurt handed her a Nirvana sticker picturing Chim-Chim, his beloved plastic monkey from *Speed Racer.* Kurt had several toy monkeys, but Chim-Chim was especially dear to him because it was so realistic—a wizened, bat-faced little creature with a long skinny tail. He had taped batteries to its back and run wires from the batteries to electrodes on its skull. On the sticker, it appeared to be eating a butterfly.

"You've got Dave Pirner damage," Courtney said.

"Who?"

She gave him a disbelieving look. "The guy from Soul Asylum. You fuckin' think you're him, right?"

"Fuck you . . . ohhh, I gotta go, there's my girlfriend."

Courtney glanced across the club at Tracy Marander, a voluptuous girl with flame-red hair for whom the caustic Nirvana song "About a Girl" was written. "She's *fat!*"

"Bitch!" Kurt shoved Courtney out of her chair and wrestled her onto the floor. They tumbled drunkenly in the morass of spilled beer and cigarette dregs. "Look at the fuckin' love-rocker from Olympia!" Courtney sneered. "Isn't he out of character!" As soon as the words had left her mouth, Kurt leaned down and kissed her.

If Kurt hadn't been with Tracy, Courtney would have taken him home that night. As it was, they wouldn't meet up again for a year and a half—and when they did, Courtney's band would be on the verge of outshining Kurt's.

Portland was getting claustrophobic. In early 1989 Jennifer Finch convinced Courtney to move back to L.A. Veteran punk Don Bolles's band Celebrity Skin was one of the hottest acts in Hollywood. Courtney had known them for years, had even written them up for a couple of music magazines. Now she turned up backstage like a dervish. She found out later that Don and Tim, the bass player, had a bet going that night: if Courtney stayed over with them, they'd made it. If she didn't, they hadn't. She stayed because she didn't have anywhere else to stay yet. During the party Celebrity Skin threw to celebrate their newfound "success," Don pulled Courtney aside. "You're gonna have to top yourself soon," he told her. "You're getting boring."

Courtney stared the forty-something scenester full in the face.

"Don? You see this dress I'm wearing?" She smoothed the black velvet over her still-ample hips. "Six months from now, three of me will be able to fit into this dress. So *shut up.*"

Don's remark stung, but it also lit a fire under her ass. She decided to give up all her sidelines—acting, clubbing, the promotion of talentless boys—and concentrate seriously on losing weight and finding a band. She placed an ad in *Flipside* and in *The Recycler,* a famous L.A. clearinghouse for hopeful musicians: "I want to start a band. My influences are Big Black, Sonic Youth, and Fleetwood Mac."

While waiting for her perfect bandmates to turn up, Courtney danced at Jumbo's Clown Room again, and also at the Seventh Veil and Star Strip, places that had refused to hire her when she was heavier. She soon quit, though: the DJs kept playing Faith No More, and she couldn't stand to think of the smirk that would grace Roddy Bottum's chiseled face if he knew Courtney Love was taking off her clothes to his band.

Impatient for things to start happening, Courtney bought her next-door neighbor Lisa a used bass. The first musician to answer her *Recycler* ad was Eric Erlandson, a twenty-seven-year-old clerk at Capitol Records who would prove to have the patience of several saints. The audition was like nothing he'd ever seen before: "It was Courtney and Lisa on bass with no drummer. I stood there playing whatever noise I could think of, and they were strumming their guitars, screaming at the top of their lungs. I thought, *Wow, this is gonna be interesting!*"

"He had a Thurston [Moore] quality about him," Courtney recalls. "He was tall, skinny, blonde. He dressed pretty cool, and he knew who Sonic Youth were." She hadn't envisioned any men in her band, but a year later she would award Eric her highest accolade: "[He] plays like a girl. Girls' playing is compassion and rage, and it can also be ugly and jarring."

At the time, she was impressed enough to call him back and set up a meeting at a coffee shop. "She called me up and talked my ear off," Eric told *Rolling Stone.* "I thought, *Oh God, oh no, what am I getting myself into?* She grabbed me and started talking, and she's like, 'I know you're the one!' And I hadn't even opened my mouth yet."

Eric was in for the long haul. After that came a lot of false starts. Lisa was kicked out for being *"beyond* deathrock." One would-be guitarist had just gotten out of jail on a mysterious felony charge; she was a Mennonite whose lyrics harped incessantly upon "the jaws of God and Death." At last they found bassist Jill Emery and drummer Caroline Rue, both of whom would remain with the band for two years.

Courtney's original intention was to call the band Sweet Baby Crystal Powered By God. Once she got over that, the name Hole came from two sources. The first was a conversation Courtney had with her mother in which Linda told her she couldn't carry a hole around inside her just because she'd suffered a problematic childhood. (*The hell I can't!* Courtney thought.) The second was a line from Euripides' tragedy *Medea* in which the title character speaks of a hole pierced through her soul. The word's sexual connotations were never the main idea, but they didn't bother Courtney either.

She began a flirtation with Falling James Moreland, who was the punk transvestite front man of a band called the Leaving Trains, and also a more-or-less-ex-boyfriend of Jennifer Finch. Jennifer, who was now in L7, didn't mind; she had a slew of other, increasingly younger boyfriends. At the time, Courtney was stripping in Hollywood. Falling James picked her up from work one night and said, "I dare you to go to Vegas and marry me."

They got really drunk on cheap casino-mixed cocktails in Las Vegas, where they were married in a quickie ceremony just before dawn. When they got back to L.A., Courtney made Moreland drop her off at Club Lingerie, where she saw L7 open for the Gun Club and told everybody what she had done.

Courtney and her friends treated the whole thing as a joke, but Falling James tried to break down her apartment door the next day, screaming, *"I'm your husband!"* Today, long after a divorce and an annulment, Falling James Moreland calls himself "the Eddie Fisher of punk rock."

"I thought I was marrying the female Johnny Rotten," he told the *New York Press* in a May 1996 interview, "and that was a political goof. Instead I got this right-wing Phyllis Diller." He labels Courtney a homophobic conservative (making no mention of her lesbian drummer, the gay men who have befriended her and worked with her for most of her life, or her own sexual experimentation) and expresses a paranoid fear of her, claiming that during their marriage she "threatened to have me beaten up when I didn't do what she wanted. I was so scared of her I caved in immediately . . . I'm [still] scared of her."

While these statements say far more about Falling James Moreland than they do about Courtney Love, they are also evidence of Courtney's state of mind. For too long she had fallen in love too easily; now she legally bound herself to a man she didn't love at all, partly as a lark, partly for the (however temporary) cachet of having the cross-dressing lead singer of a popular band as a husband. Though he would coproduce Hole's first single, Courtney and Falling James eventually became so estranged that, seven years later, he could still say a thing like "Most people would want to kill themselves just waking up to her."

However brief and inexplicable the union may have been, Courtney soon came to her senses. She filed a petition with the Superior Court of California to have the marriage annulled. The legal effect of the court order granting the annulment is to render the marriage void *ab initio,* a nullity, something that never happened.

"It was the stupidest thing I ever did," she admits of the marriage. What made her do it? Was she proving to herself that she could use men as easily as they had used her? Did the scent of impending success stimulate her longtime self-destructive urge?

As anyone might have expected, Courtney also became involved with Eric Erlandson. Though they were lovers for a year and a half, no one ever really thought of them as a couple. "It's weird that no one asked," Eric told *Kerrang!* magazine, "but we kept it pretty tight. I don't recommend for anybody to go out with someone they're in a band with, but it's one of those things that just happens sometimes. You work together and you end up sleeping together. It's a part of life, but the problem is that continuing afterwards is really, really hard. We both hate and love each other now because we know each other so well."

Eric was, and remains, a calming influence on Courtney. Their relationship wasn't terribly romantic, but it was more *sensible* than any other she'd had. Unlike her previous boyfriends, he accepted her moods and whims and tirades with equanimity. He possesses a serenity that makes all manner of abuse seem to roll off his back. When Courtney turned him on to Buddhism, he took to it immediately.

Hole played their first show at Raji's in Hollywood, opening for L7, and were soon getting booked at punk bars and clubs all over L.A. Many of their early shows didn't live up to Courtney's exacting standards. "I started to play this new thing," she wrote of one gig, "and NO ONE JOINED IN, <u>NO ONE,</u> oh God it was so catastrophic and gross. Like 3 retarded children." But they were good enough to attract interest from several independent labels.

The Long Beach–based label Sympathy for the Record Industry released Hole's first single, "Retard Girl" backed with "Phone Bill Song" and "Johnnies in the Bathroom," in March 1990. Pressed on pale pink vinyl and featuring a cover photo of

Kat Bjelland showing her panties, the single included a leaflet that read in part

> GAG. 1. Don't have children with people who will repulse you in the future. . . . I AM FREE TO VOMIT MY OWN BEING.

◇

After "Retard Girl" came out, Hole went on a limited tour, play-

ing small clubs and bars all over the country. On this tour Court-

ney met Billy Corgan, the twenty-three-year-old lead singer for

Smashing Pumpkins, whose debut single "I Am One" had been

released in 1989 by Chicago label Limited Potential. Rumor had

it that they'd met at the house of a drug dealer, but in reality,

Billy offered to put up Hole at his apartment when they played

Chicago.

Billy was an odd combination of sensitive soul and control freak. Dark-haired and dark-eyed with pale, pale skin, he was an inch shorter than Courtney and had terrible posture and a little potbelly. "Billy Pumpkin" would never be one of her pretty boys —indeed, her description of his body would later inspire a jealous Kurt Cobain to label him "the pear-shaped box." Courtney wasn't physically attracted to him at first, but his sharp intellect and casual alpha-male dominance drew her.

Like Courtney, Billy had been handed around to various relatives as a child, had been a pariah at school, had never felt truly wanted anywhere. "Why did you have me if you didn't want me?" he has challenged his parents in the press. "Why did you have me if you weren't going to take care of me?"

Though Billy had had the same on-again, off-again girlfriend for years, he and Courtney became very tight. He wasn't quite the soul mate she knew she'd find someday, but he was a hell of a lot closer than Rozz, and by this time Eric Erlandson had become more like a brother to her. Also, there was a factor at work in their relationship that Courtney hadn't experienced before: Billy Corgan was worthy competition. Now that male musicians were taking her seriously, Courtney found that she thrived on competition. From then on, she could never sustain a serious romance with anyone whose talents didn't rival her own.

Speaking of competition, her once-close relationship with Kat Bjelland was beginning to haunt her. They had always been influenced by the same books and movies (Carroll Baker in *Baby Doll*, often credited with inspiring their "kinderwhore" look, was a big favorite). They had traded clothes and riffs and lyrics and, occasionally, men. Now Babes in Toyland's first album, *Spanking Machine*, was out, and Babes were touring Europe with Sonic Youth. Courtney felt that Kat was pulling ahead of her.

"She is now starting to bother me and it is my own fault," Courtney wrote to a friend.

I didn't spawn her and I didn't create her ingenuity and it's not my fault that she is shorter and cuter than me, but it is starting to bother me nonetheless that she is making headway on my shtick. Simply because my own shtick is suddenly her shtick. It is ugly. I taught her my shtick, month after month, year after year, and voila! What did I expect? My shoes don't seem like my shoes anymore. I look at a dress and wonder what it would look like on her before I buy it. I hate my guitar, I want a different one. She says it's destiny. Feels like penance.

Later, she would have a different take on this feud, which Neal Karlen, in his book *Babes in Toyland*, called the War of the *Schmatte*. "I felt molested and stolen from constantly," she said in late 1994. "It wasn't until a female friend not only wrote about me but also took some of my own persona from me that I changed my outlook. Seeing enough worth in my persona to take it from me. It was a great compliment, it was a gift. Not my soul, but my persona; [Kat] took this and created her own world with it. It really moved me to get off my ass and do it myself. I thank her."

In winter of 1990, Courtney started having long phone conversations with Dave Grohl, Nirvana's drummer and one of Jennifer Finch's boyfriends. During one of their talks, Courtney let slip that she had a crush on Kurt, whom she'd nicknamed "pixie meat." Dave told Courtney that Kurt liked her too, and that Kurt was miserable after a recent breakup with his girlfriend, Bikini Kill drummer Tobi Vail.

"I was definitely looking for someone I could spend quite a few years with," Kurt told Michael Azerrad, author of the definitive Nirvana history *Come As You Are*. "I wanted that security and I knew that it wasn't with [Tobi]. I was just tired of not finding the right mate. I'd been looking all my life. I just got tired of trying to have a girlfriend that I knew that I wouldn't eventually spend more than a couple of months with. I've always been old-fashioned in that respect . . . I wish I was capable of just playing the field, but I always wanted more than that." Tracy Marander hadn't been "artistic" enough for him. Tobi Vail was only twenty-one, too young to think about settling down.

Courtney was still seeing Billy, but she didn't believe the relationship was going anywhere: Billy had a steady girlfriend in Chicago *and* fucked around on the road whenever he pleased. Encouraged by the breakup and by Dave's revelation, she put together a special package for Dave to give to Kurt.

She had been collecting heart-shaped boxes for years. She selected a Victorian one of silk and lace, spritzed the interior with her perfume, and packed it full of tiny exquisite things: a handful of seashells and baby pinecones, dried tea roses, a doll, a set of miniature teacups. She raised it to her face, breathed deeply of its fragrance, exhaled into it as if her breath could carry a voodoo spell. Then she fitted the lid on carefully, tied it with a ribbon, and entrusted it to Dave's care.

Kurt never responded. But Courtney never gave up easily.

◇

By the beginning of 1991, Courtney had already been keeping

notes on Hole's debut album for months: adding and discarding

possible songs, choosing the title, considering artwork and design.

True to her character, she intended to retain as much creative

control as possible over every aspect of the intricate record-

making process.

On the first day of the new year, she drafted a letter to Kim

Gordon of Sonic Youth:

Dear Miss Kim:

Here is a tape of our Sub Pop 7 inch which is supposed to come out in a week or two. We are looking to make an LP in the next month. We had a meeting thinking who to try for a producer and besides the fact that we would prefer working with a woman, we really like the way the STP record sounds & all admire your body of work quite hugingly & slenchingly. If you are at all interested I will give you a rehearsal tape. We would be completely honored and stoked.

This humble missive was decorated with little hearts and signed, "Thank You, Courtney Love."

On the back of the page she listed the accoutrements of her kinderwhore look, which she was deep into by now:

Used to use Rembrandt [toothpaste] until I found out they sponsor the Rush Limbaugh show. I like tooth powder. Xtra pair undies (high waisted white cotton from Woolworth's), Carmex, 3–4 baby barrettes, Great Lash Mascara & YSL Moss Mascara, 2 clean Max Factor powder puffs, Xtra vintage white slip, Bobbi Brown taupe eyeshadow, Christian Dior Holiday Red pencil, Wet'n'Wild Shiny Frosty Pink, my fourth pair of Marilyn rhinestone shades from Patricia Fields ($98 and I keep breaking them).

The kinderwhore style developed by Courtney and Kat dovetailed so neatly with the burgeoning Riot Grrrl movement that for a while Hole and Babes in Toyland were thought of as proto–Riot Grrrl bands. But Riot Grrrl's true roots were at Evergreen State College in Olympia, Washington, where four young women launched a feminist zine called *Bikini Kill*, then a band by the same name. Expanding by a grassroots network of zines and bands, Riot Grrrl set out to dismantle the patriarchal power structure, and to hell with learning the three basic chords first.

The original Riot Grrrls were militant punk feminists, but as with any trend, the "look" filtered into the general population. Soon teenage girls all over the country were wearing plastic barrettes, carrying Hello Kitty lunch boxes, coming to concerts with words like SLUT and BITCH scrawled on their bodies in lipstick or Magic Marker. Courtney wondered whether these girls understood the irony of this look, or if they were just being encouraged to appear young, cute, and harmless. She told *Melody Maker* that she feared Riot Grrrl had become too "teensy, weensy, widdle, cutie. I think the reason the media is so excited about it is because it's saying females are inept, females are naive, females are innocent, clumsy, bratty . . . [But] I wore those small dresses [too], and sometimes I regret it."

In March 1991, Sub Pop released Hole's second single, "Dicknail" backed with "Burn Black." It was an arrival of sorts: Sub Pop had put out most of the music that inspired Courtney to return to the art form. At the same time, they were recording their debut album, coproduced by Kim Gordon and Don Fleming (of Gumball). *Pretty on the Inside* is often described by non-enthusiasts of punk as difficult or even impossible to listen to. Listeners who cut their teeth on bands like Sonic Youth and the Minutemen may disagree, but the album was certainly hard-edged enough to satisfy Courtney's craving for street credibility.

"When I was composing *Pretty on the Inside,* I had just been kicked out of Babes in Toyland, and I had a real chip on my shoulder," she said after the album was released. "I was like, 'I'm gonna be the angriest girl in the world, fuck you!' I didn't want to have a crack in my surface and put something jangly on there. I really wish that I had put something pretty on there. I mean, I'm glad people don't expect much from me, but at the same time, I wish that they had an inkling that I had an inkling how to write."

In May, Courtney saw Kurt backstage at a Butthole Surfers/ Redd Kross/L7 show at the Palladium. She punched him in the stomach (perhaps for not acknowledging her heart-shaped box, perhaps just out of affection), he punched back, and they fell on the floor wrestling. "It was a mating ritual for dysfunctional people," she says.

Nirvana was in town recording *Nevermind* at Sound City, the same studio where Fleetwood Mac had recorded Courtney's beloved *Rumours*. It turned out that Kurt was living only a block away from Courtney. Nothing more happened the night of the Palladium show, but shortly thereafter, Courtney got a call at six in the morning. It was Kurt. "Can I come over? Do you have any drugs?"

Courtney and Eric were living in the same apartment complex, and they still shared a bed sometimes, though their relationship was purely platonic by now. "No, I don't have any drugs, and it's six in the fucking morning, and I'm on a date."

"Well, just let me come over."

"Well . . . okay." She kept her voice nonchalant until they hung up, then shook Eric awake. "Eric! Go upstairs!"

"Why?"

"Because pixie meat's coming over."

Eric knew all about the girl-boner she'd been nurturing for Kurt. Still only half-awake, he dragged himself upstairs and crawled into his own bed.

Kurt arrived with a bottle of Hycomine cough syrup. "You're a pussy," Courtney told him. "You shouldn't drink that, it's bad for your stomach." (She already knew about his stomach problems, which were chronic but not yet crippling.) Then she produced a bottle of Vicodin extra-strength. "We bonded over pharmaceuticals," Courtney recalls. But, though they had sex, they didn't really bond that morning. Despite his later claim that he'd been looking for this all his life, Kurt was reluctant to get into another serious relationship so soon after the failure of his

112

last one, and he knew any relationship with Courtney would have to be serious.

"She seemed like poison because I'd just gotten out of the last relationship that I didn't even want to be in," he told Michael Azerrad. "I was determined to be a bachelor for a few months. I just had to be. But I knew that I liked Courtney so much right away that it was a really hard struggle to stay away from her for so many months. It was harder than shit. During that time that I attempted to be a bachelor and sow my oats and live the bachelor rock'n'roll lifestyle, I didn't end up fucking anybody or having a good time at all."

Courtney had plenty on her plate without trying to chase down a man who couldn't decide whether he was interested in her or not. Their album was finished, and they had plans to tour Europe with Mudhoney. In June, Hole received their first rave review (titled "Foreign Orifice") from *Melody Maker* writer Everett True, who'd caught their show at Hollywood's Club Lingerie:

> Courtney Love, singer with Hole, tells me I write like a lover. A mean lover. Courtney Love would make a lousy lover—she'd fuck you once, make you fall in love and then leave you for dead. Still, any experience is better than none at all. I guess. As Courtney would say, fuck it! You wanna go roll around in mud all day, you wanna go masturbate non-stop, you wanna go be a slut for four years? Fuck it! You can't rape the willing!
>
> Hole. Yeah, right. Tonight in Hollywood, amid films of strippers and tales of anguish and exhilaration I witness the best . . . no, scratch that. Tonight I witness the *only* rock'n'roll band in the world. Something to do with equal amounts energy, luck, pain, passion, anger, and the three major chords, I reckon. Courtney Love has been alternately described as the "illegitimate love child of Madonna and Lydia Lunch" and "the

drunk man's Madonna." Accurate descriptions, both, if a little too glib for my liking . . .

[T]onight Hole cause me to lose sight of where I am and my feet to clump heavily back and forth the way they do only due to fatigue or the most extreme noise conditions. And if I'm not in love this time then I never fucking will be. Put simply: awesome. Of course, bands being bands and dumb stupid creatures who wouldn't hurt a fly unless it came up and peek-a-booed them on the nose, Hole reckon they've never sounded worse, roundly whipping the drummer for her sins and bad timing afterward. Eric tries to throw his guitar at our brave photographer and that's that. Jesus! That was *bad?* Let's not throw the good at me too fast, huh?

Hole are a fucking revelation.

So let's talk about the songs. *Songs,* right? "Teenage Whore" is pretty much the most unsettling thing I've heard since Patti Smith uncovered "Piss Factory" and then fucked off to become a middle-aged housewife, only it's way more personal. Like, you *feel* for her mother, when Courtney screams at us about how she got thrown out of the house for fucking around. "Garbadge Man" (note spelling) has the sexiest ending since Bongwater's Ann Magnuson whined *"I wa-a-ant one"* at the end of "Nick Cave Dolls"—and that's some sexy, I'm telling you. "Good Sister/Bad Sister" is Beat Happening if they'd grown up feminist, over-sexed, and *wired.* "Baby Doll" is lamest, cos it sounds like those middle-aged middle-class jerk-offs Sonic Youth. But what the hell. The sight of Eric and Jill rampaging possessed (and believe me, you ain't seen no possession 'til you seen Hole) across the strip-club stage more

114

than compensates for that. And Eric plays Black Sabbath better than any white boy I've seen.

Oh, hell. Let's leave it here. Hole are sexy, happening, possessed, and brutally, brutally honest. They make Bret Easton Ellis sound like a two-bit prankster. I came to L.A. thinking I knew everything there was to know about rock. I left a virtual beginner.

Hole are the *only* band in the world. It's the only way to feel.

After wrapping up *Nevermind,* Nirvana spent the summer touring Europe with Sonic Youth. Hole's tour with Mudhoney followed a few weeks later, playing many of the same clubs, and Courtney reported that Kurt had left cryptic graffiti for her in all the dressing rooms. At England's Reading Festival, Courtney was getting drunk with Kat and Kim Gordon when filmmaker Dave Markey, shooting the documentary *1991: The Year Punk Broke,* appeared backstage. Courtney looked straight into the camera and slurred, "Kurt Cobain makes my heart stop. But he's a shit."

He almost proved it later in the tour, when they met up at a club in London. *"I'm* going to be a rock star soon," he told Courtney.

"You are *not.*"

"Yes I am. I'm going to be a big rock star. I'm going to buy antiques—really *expensive* antiques for my *wife."*

Shortly thereafter, Kurt left the club with two voluptuous English girls, making sure that Courtney noticed. Unwilling to let him think she cared, Courtney yelled after him, "I hope you get *fucked!"*

She'd been watching Mudhoney's Mark Arm stage-dive almost every night, casting his long skinny body into the waiting sea of arms, and the practice intrigued her. At the Astoria in London, she finally took the plunge—and regretted it. At once hundreds of hands were all over her body, groping, tearing, *invading*. When she got back to the stage, she was almost naked and in tears. She treated the crowd to a torrent of verbal abuse, and then she smashed her guitar. "It broke into a million pieces," she told *Siren* soon afterward. "Like, the full rock thing. I destroyed it. I wasn't thinking. I can be primal. I can do it and not intellectualize breaking my guitar in front of sixteen hundred people—*fuck you!* So many things went wrong, and I was just so mad. I probably did about five thousand dollars' worth of damage that night."

"i was returned to the stage basically naked, dirty hands had been all over me . . . etc. . . ." she would post on the Internet years later, recalling the incident. ". . . WHAT IS ETC.? well it just was etc., i saw a photo of that moment, i was smiling, pretending everything was ok, i guess, it started to dawn on me that this had been my own fault—for bleaching and makeupping and wearing a 'little' dress . . ."

Pretty on the Inside was released by Caroline Records in September 1991. Dedicated to Rob Ritter, a musician friend who'd died of a heroin overdose in 1990, it had a blurry cover photo of the band on a hot-pink background, a disturbingly effective back-cover painting by Jill Emery, and a lyric sheet partly handwritten by Courtney and decorated with cutout pictures of dolls, sacred hearts, and women's bodies.

The album was unanimously well reviewed. Edwin Pouncey of *New Musical Express* compared it to American punk classics like Patti Smith's *Horses* and the debut albums of the Ramones, the New York Dolls, and Television. While most of the reviews concentrated on Hole's arresting front woman, Pouncey gave due credit to the other band members. "Courtney's wild woman blues holler (shades of Janis Joplin at her bourbon-broken best) is equally matched by the instrumental side of Hole, a chinkless wall of sonic concrete that stands up to anything Courtney can throw at it."

"Teenage Whore" was chosen *Spin's* Single of the Week, and the album made it onto the "Adventure Picks" list of *CMJ*, an influential magazine aimed at college and independent radio stations. Elizabeth Wurtzel (author of *Prozac Nation*) wrote in *The New Yorker*, "*Pretty on the Inside* is such a cacophony—full of such grating, abrasive, and unpleasant sludges of noise—that very few people are likely to get through it once, let alone give it the repeated listenings it needs for you to discover that it's probably the most compelling album to have been released in 1991."

A week later, Nirvana's *Nevermind* came out. Given an initial pressing of 50,000 copies, which was how many *Bleach* had sold, it would soon be selling more than that *per day*. But by then the band was on tour and had little idea of their own sales figures. In Athens, Georgia, they partied at R.E.M. guitarist Peter Buck's Victorian mansion. Buck's then-wife Barrie, who managed the 40 Watt Club, noticed that Kurt couldn't stop talking about the singer from Hole. When Courtney happened to talk to Barrie Buck a couple of weeks later, Barrie passed along this interesting bit of news.

On October 10, Courtney managed to scam a plane ticket to Chicago off a record-industry manager. She told him she wanted to see Nirvana at the Metro, but she actually thought they had played there two nights before; she really only wanted to see Billy Corgan. Unfortunately, she hadn't told Billy she was coming. When Courtney arrived at his apartment, his girlfriend was there. The enraged woman started throwing shoes out the window, and Billy told Courtney to leave.

"Okay, fine," she sobbed, "I'll go see Nirvana." (She still thought they had played two nights before, but she also knew that Billy was jealous of Kurt.) "Where's the Metro?"

Billy pointed her the wrong way, and soon she found herself deep in a burned-out crack ghetto. She'd left some of her luggage at Billy's place in the confusion, and all she had was a bag of lingerie. She spent her last ten dollars on a cab ride to the Metro, where it turned out Nirvana really were playing. "Can I stay at your hotel tonight?" she asked Kurt.

"Why?"

"Because Billy Pumpkin kicked me out, of all things."

"Oh, God, that's so gross that you go out with him."

"I don't go out with him anymore. But yeah, you're right." Courtney started to cry.

"What's wrong?"

"I don't think anyone's ever gonna, like, love me."

"Well, no one's ever gonna love me either."

"Oh, good . . ."

Their eyes met and locked, and that was the irrevocable moment.

Courtney made herself call Billy. She knew something special was going to happen with Kurt, something more than either of them had expected before, and she wanted to make a clean break with Billy first. "I don't want to do this sleazy," she told Billy. "I'm not going to do what you did. I'm going to be with Kurt now, but I can fly and meet him later if you want to talk face-to-face. Do you want to see me today?" (It was already well past midnight.)

"I have to see my brother today. Maybe I'll see you tonight."

"Billy, fuck you, I flew out here to see you. I'm not coming back. I'm not going to give myself half-assed to Kurt."

"Fuck it," said Billy. "Just do whatever you want."

Courtney hung up, went back to Nirvana's hotel, the Days Inn on Diversey, and got drunk with them. Kurt tried on some of Courtney's lingerie, a sight that charmed her beyond all control. Kurt was sharing a room with Dave Grohl, and when the new couple started making noisy love on Kurt's bed, Dave had to go sleep with the soundman.

The next week, Courtney had to fly to Germany for a show. She sent Kurt a long fax that began with a shrewd analysis ("No one has a right to make you feel guilty about what you deserve. I know that you need someone to make you feel guilty so that you can pretend you don't deserve it, because you are so horrified of what you are capable of, because inside you are actually gloating, or not even that, <u>sub</u>-gloating, smirking, going <u>duh</u>") and progressed through punk rock bravado ("I just asked a German for a cigarette and she said <u>NO.</u> That bitch, I want her to die") to flippant remorse ("I wish I could erase at least half the people I ever fucked because it was a waste of eggs and milk and Monistat cream"). It was signed "Your Personal Goddess."

Then she flew home and they began keeping constant company. Kurt and Courtney would never spend more than a few weeks away from each other for the next two and a half years.

◇

Kurt Donald Cobain was born on February 20, 1967, in the industrial town of Aberdeen, Washington. He was the first child of Wendy Fradenburg Cobain, a housewife, and Donald Cobain, a mechanic. Wendy's brother and sister played in bands, and Kurt developed an interest in music very early on; pictures of him whaling on a toy guitar were taken just before his second birthday.[1]

---

[1] Don Cobain may have gifted his son with a darker legacy. The family has a history of suicide by gunshot. In 1979, Kurt's great-uncle Burle Cobain killed himself with a shot to the abdomen. In 1984, Burle's brother Kenneth followed suit with a shot to the head. Rumors of more suicides extend far back into the history of this Irish-American family; Courtney has referred to "the Cobain curse."

Manic, rebellious, and hypercreative, he was prescribed Ritalin and then sedatives at age seven, without much success (arguably so, according to what one thinks his parents and doctors were trying to achieve—if they intended to make him a happier and more "normal" child, they failed). The following year his parents divorced, which seems to have sent him spiraling into a lifelong depression. "It destroyed his life," Wendy Cobain (now Wendy O'Connor) said later. "He changed completely. I think he was ashamed. And he became very inward—he just held everything. He became very shy."

After the divorce, Kurt was shuttled from parent to parent, and eventually to various relatives. Like Hank Harrison, Donald Cobain was absent emotionally, if not physically; like Linda, Wendy O'Connor was too traumatized by the events of her own life to take care of her firstborn child. Kurt ran away from home a number of times, lived at friends' houses or under a bridge, hated school and often blew it off, learned to play guitar, got into rock and then punk.

("He was a closet deathrocker," Courtney would reveal later. "Some of the art he bought is so goth it's unbelievable. If you actually listen to Nirvana, some of it's almost kind of like Bauhaus. But he would *never* admit that. He made a list of his favorite records and I didn't even see Zeppelin on there. Or Devo or Bauhaus. It was all obscure bands . . . That was one of our biggest fights. I was like, 'That list, why are you doing that?'—it was going to be in the Azerrad book. He's like, 'So kids will buy it.' I'm like, 'Kids are gonna buy Saccharine Trust and *like* it?' But you can't even *play* his fuckin' Bauhaus records anymore, they're so scratched up.")

When drugs entered his life, Kurt took to them much more easily than Courtney had. Courtney enjoyed drugs, but she'd always been too much of a control freak to let them run her life; she'd done them for fun, for companionship, because they were there. Kurt did drugs because they made him feel better. He had always suffered from vague malaises; he had chronic bronchitis and a minor curvature of the spine, and the mysterious, agonizing stomach problems that would plague him for the rest of his life. Opiates embraced him. He got addicted to Percodans while he was still in high school, kicked them without too much pain, then tried heroin.

Though he didn't develop a habit right away—there was no steady supply in Aberdeen—it was love at first shot. He'd always known he would try heroin, and once he'd done it, he knew he would do it again whenever he got the chance. By the time Courtney met him, he was shooting up often.

Kurt's former girlfriends hadn't reacted well to his drug use. Tracy had been frightened by it, and Tobi was disgusted—no one did hard drugs in healthy, happy Olympia, or if they did, they didn't talk about it. Courtney accepted it as a natural part of his life, especially when he told her that heroin relieved his pain. That was something she could relate to.

Kurt was fragile, bird-boned, exquisitely wrought. Thinner than she'd been in years, Courtney still outweighed him by a good ten pounds. Along with his passive demeanor, this made her feel very tender toward him, almost maternal. She hadn't felt so close to anyone since Geneva from reform school, Geneva her almost-lover, and she convinced herself that there was some psychic connection between the two. Perhaps her love for Kurt could assuage some of the grief she still felt for Geneva.

"In that nice clean room we went so deep," she wrote of staying with Kurt in some anonymous hotel.

> It was so cozy and dirty and cool. He told me he loved me and I know that he does. It just feels so unreal—those silvery eyes burning holes into me. It made me want to protect him, keep him from people that would hurt him/use him. . . . I want to spend a long time with him. Last night I could not sleep and I half

dreamt of us making love and I woke up crying with a
GUT ache, and I had to call him, I felt like my heart
was going to <u>break</u>, but then I talked to him and I was
so <u>happy</u>. SO HAPPY."

By November 1991, Hole and Nirvana were both touring in
Europe. *Nevermind* had already gone platinum in the U.S., and
Nirvana seemed to be falling apart in classic rocket-to-fame
mode. Dave Grohl was said to have developed claustrophobia and
a sudden fear of flying. Krist Novoselic stayed drunk on expensive
Bordeaux. Stomach pains and bronchitis racked Kurt's thin body;
he was chain-smoking, guzzling liquor and cough syrup, vomiting
before shows.

When Courtney could be there, her presence reassured
Kurt. But she often felt ambivalent about being there to
reassure the star, even if he was the love of her life. "I am
100/th as famous," she wrote. "I have sold about 100/th the
records. I am so stripped so pinned I want you you you you, I
want to hold you be your Mother x Whore, you be my man x
boy girl girl girl weirdest 2 girls in the world. We got money.
Fuck you."

On the other hand, the relationship (and perhaps the competition) stoked her creativity. She was writing notebooks full of
lyrics, including most of the songs that would later be on *Live
Through This*. Around Thanksgiving, in Amsterdam, they did
heroin together for the first time, wallowing in the childlike full-
body pleasure of it.

As Nirvana's fame swelled, Courtney's jealousy became tinged
with fear for Kurt. She had seen plenty of fame casualties, and
she didn't intend to let him be one. On December 5, lying in bed
together, they decided to get married.

Nirvana's tour ended the next night in France. Kurt flew back
to Seattle and stayed high until Courtney got home later in De-

cember. They moved into Eric Erlandson's L.A. apartment and went shopping for engagement rings. Courtney got an antique ruby, Kurt a filigreed gold band.

That December, Courtney suffered the loss of an old friend. On the nineteenth, Hole played the Whiskey A Go Go. Joe Cole, a former Hole roadie who had filmed the band's first tour, attended the show with his good friend Henry Rollins. On their way home, Rollins and Cole were held up by two gunmen bent on robbery, and Cole was shot dead.

Courtney didn't hear about it until the next night. She and Kurt had just picked up his visa for Nirvana's upcoming Japanese tour, and they stopped off at the Hamburger Hamlet, where many of their friends hung out. A girl named Marsha was there with goth-rock legend Siouxsie Sioux. Courtney had never met Siouxsie before and was ready to be impressed, but Marsha said, "Did you hear what happened to Joe last night?"

"No, what?"

"Well, he got shot."

"Is he okay?"

"No, he's dead."

Joe Cole was only the second close friend whose death Courtney had experienced. The first had been Rob Ritter of the band 45 Grave, but that had been from heroin, and as awful as it seems to think it, a junkie's death never comes as a total surprise. Joe's death was different: random, huge, and scary. *Live Through This* would be dedicated to his memory.

The living arrangement with Eric didn't last long. Soon Kurt and Courtney were living in a series of hotels, staying in bed as much as possible, doing brown Mexican heroin that Kurt had to shoot into Courtney's arm—she still couldn't hit her own vein.

Now that Kurt had someone to share with, to wallow with, to have sloppy, lazy, heroin-drenched sex with, he was using more heavily than ever before. In the Nirvana camp, blame fell on Courtney, even to the extent of suggesting that she had turned him on to the drug.

"It's like this," Courtney told Michael Azerrad. " 'Hey, you know what? I just sold a million fuckin' records and I got a million bucks and I'm going to share it with you and let's get high!' . . .

"[Heroin]'s the drug that makes you sleepy and happy. That's the drug you do if you're in a fuckin' five-star hotel and you can order all the goddamn room service that you want and you can just lay in bed and drool all over yourself because you've got a million bucks in the bank. That's the drug you do when you want to be a kid forever."

If this explanation made management nervous, Kurt and Courtney's interview in the April 1992 issue of *Sassy* must have sent them into fits. "In the last couple of months," Kurt started off, "I've gotten engaged and my attitude has changed drastically, and I can't believe how much happier I am and how even less career-oriented I am. At times I even forget I'm in a band, I'm so blinded by love. I know that sounds embarrassing, but it's true. I could give up the band right now. It doesn't matter." They talked about the Victorian house they planned to buy in Seattle, and about the baby they wanted to have.

The interview had been conducted in January, when Nirvana was in New York to tape an appearance on *Saturday Night Live.* "We went on a binge," Courtney said later. "We did a lot of drugs. We got pills and then we went down to Alphabet City and Kurt wore a hat, I wore a hat, and we copped some dope."

"People just wait in a line," Kurt marveled. "Lawyers, businesspeople in three-piece suits, junkies, lowlifes, all different kinds of people."

Back in L.A., they rented an apartment on North Spaulding Avenue in the Fairfax district and proceeded to decorate it with doll heads, toy monkeys, heart-shaped boxes, cigarette burns, and graffiti. One night after an argument, Courtney scrawled MY BEST FRIEND on the wall to remind Kurt of their true relationship. "I just got up and got drugs and listened to music and painted and played guitar," Kurt said of this period. "It was recuperation. I'd been on tour seven months. I needed to do that."

Pretty on the Inside was listed as one of *Melody Maker*'s top twenty albums, and "Teenage Whore" was a top-twenty single in England. By indie-rock standards, Hole was kicking ass. But living with the most successful rock star in the world could dent anyone's self-confidence. Courtney had been struggling with this dilemma since Europe. She was proud of Kurt and thought he deserved every bit of his fame and fortune. But *she* deserved it just as much. She had come this far on her own determination and talent. She was damned if she was going to be perceived as grabbing onto someone else's coattails now.

And then she was just damned.

In late January, she found out she was pregnant.

CHAPTER FOURTEEN

◇

Would it have two heads? would it be helpless? Courtney asked

herself, but knew she had to have this baby. There was no way

she could destroy this mixture of herself and Kurt.

For one thing, even then, she knew Kurt didn't intend to live

a long life. She intended to tether him to this world for as

many years as possible, but his body was so fragile and tense,

his grasp of his own talent so tenuous, his mind so full of

demons. Courtney was afraid that if she aborted this pregnancy, she might not have the chance to conceive another child with him.

A teratologist they consulted assured who told them that heroin use in the first trimester of pregnancy causes no known harm to the developing fetus. ("But tell that to an American housewife," Kurt said. "You can't expect anyone to believe it.") Courtney could afford to take it slow and easy. Their fears were allayed, and they decided proceed with detox therapy and keep their "Bean" (named for her shape on the sonogram).

They checked into a Holiday Inn and delivered themselves into the care of a detox doctor. Soon the bathroom stank of their violent illness. Courtney passed the time writing voluminous letters, including this *Bell Jar*–esque one to a friend:

> I have the best taste in this town. My bedroom is peach. Faux Victorian. I finally have an eiderdown quilt. 27 years. I deserve fresh flowers. . . . I can barely write even this I am so uninspired. God I need all the help I can get. . . .
>
> Here we are the corporate power grunge couple and everyone is already bored of us. We're an institution already. He's a bowl of cereal. Very mysterious. . . . I want neckrubs so bad that I don't even mind giving them.
>
> Someone asked Janet [Billig, Hole's manager] if I'd LOST MY DRIVE. I don't know how to drive. . . . I lay prone, gutted, desperate, and empty, I swear, soulsick, not dead because of my taste and love of texture and smell but almost dead. This is the most I've written in over a month. . . . I just vomit violently and try to pretend this hasn't happened to me. I love him. We lock like a locket.

Two days after they got out of detox, Nirvana flew off to tour Australia. Seeking relief from a flare-up of his stomach pain, Kurt promptly (and, he claimed, accidentally) got hooked on opiates again. "I think I'm going to get some kind of stomach medicine and the doctor just assumes that I'd just recently gotten off of heroin and I'm going through detox and I'm on tour, so I'd better do what Keith Richard would have done and take methadone. It's called Physeptone in Australia, so I thought they were just stomach pills," he explained to Azerrad. Stomach pills more effective—and a lot more fun—than any he'd had before.

Courtney joined the tour in Japan. She bought a notebook labeled "AMERICAN FLAVOR (Excellent Stationery, Narrow Lines, This note book for the use of students. It have various purposes. Have a nice your college life!)" and recorded her feelings in the last days before her marriage:

> I'm nauseous on the bullet train sitting next to K Cobain. Torturing myself in fine pointy ways. My fame. ha ha. It's a weapon, kiss my ass, just like morning sickness. . . . It's private but I hate my talent more and more I think it's worthless and I don't care. Could it just be the commercial effect of too many sales and a semi-freak accident semi-meant to be but I'm starting to think I can't sing can't write that esteem is at an all-time low and it isn't his fault. God how could it be . . . Don't you dare dismiss me just because I married a ROCKSTAR.

On February 24, 1992, Kurt and Courtney were married in Waikiki, Hawaii. Courtney wore a diaphanous white dress that had once belonged to Frances Farmer. Kurt wore blue plaid pajamas, love beads, and a woven Guatemalan purse. They carried identical pink and white bouquets, but only Kurt was high. ("I wasn't *very* high, though. I just did a little teeny bit just so I wouldn't get sick," Kurt told Michael Azerrad.) The ceremony was conducted by a nondenominational female minister. In attendance were Dave Grohl and a few members of Nirvana's road crew. Conspicuously *not* in attendance were Krist Novoselic and his wife Shelli. Courtney couldn't stand Shelli and had banned her from the wedding. Krist said he wasn't coming if his wife wasn't welcome.

"It was *our* choice," claimed Shelli Novoselic in *Come As You Are*. "It was weird because I knew what was going on and I knew that she was pregnant and I had a real objection to her doing drugs while she was pregnant. Maybe at that point, maybe she was, maybe she wasn't. I don't know, but we all *assumed*. I didn't agree with it and I didn't agree with Kurt being so fucked up all the time and I just decided I wasn't going to go."

Back in L.A., Courtney sketched fetuses in her notebook, wrote more lyrics ("Plump," with lines like "I don't do the dishes / I throw them in the crib," must surely date from this period), and went to work putting her band back together. Jill Emery and Caroline Rue had both left. Kurt recommended drummer Patty Schemel, formerly of Seattle band Sybil, whom Courtney and Eric decided to hire immediately. Bassist Leslie Hardy would play a few shows and appear on one single, "My Beautiful Son," but Hole kept auditioning bass players throughout her tenure. Their favorite was Kristen Pfaff of Minneapolis band Janitor Joe, but she wasn't eager to abandon her gig or her hometown.

Courtney made lists of things she wanted for her and Kurt's Victorian house in Seattle. The swans, peacocks, potbellied pigs, and trellis of pink tea roses remained dreams, but they got the wisteria, the turtles, the water lilies, the greenhouse for growing orchids, and eventually the Remington twenty-gauge shotgun.

Meanwhile, in their apartment on North Spaulding, Kurt did drugs in a locked closet under the staircase. "I knew I was tempting [Courtney] all the time," he told Azerrad. "I was high all the time. I just had to keep doing it. I didn't have it out of my system. I knew if I quit then, I'd end up doing it again for at least the next couple of years all the time. I figured I'd just burn myself out of it because I hadn't experienced the full junkie feeling yet. I was still healthy. I didn't find myself just sitting in the house and nodding off and sleeping. I was always doing something artistic. I got a lot of paintings done and wrote a lot of songs."

(Kurt destroyed much of his artwork, but his surviving paintings, sculptures, and collages are as savage as his voice. There is an antique glass case full of jointed wooden figures that appear to be coming alive, flailing in agony. There is a Victorian baby doll in a pink dress, the front of its porcelain skull cut away to reveal the organs of the cranium, including a single eye in the middle of the forehead. There is a gold-framed canvas with a sky-blue background and a disturbing quintet of figures: an armless cat, two stick-thin puppets jerked by their strings, a tiny angel or fairy, and a ghostly glowing figure without a face. Coming from the latter's lower left abdomen is a banner that reads, "HYPER-PYLAURIC FISTULA, rectal abcess, GASTROENTERITIS, conjunctivitis, SPINABIFFIDA." There are, of course, the liner of *Nevermind*, the front and back covers of *In Utero*, and the front cover of *Incesticide*.)

He wrote most of *In Utero* during this time, with Courtney as a captive audience and sometime collaborator (she wrote some of "Pennyroyal Tea"). He never saw his band. Krist railed about Kurt's drug use to other people. Dave kept quiet and stayed away. No one wanted to see the expectant parents. They lived in a quiet world of their own, the three of them: Courtney tripping out on pregnancy beyond the first trimester, the Bean listening to muffled guitar riffs, Kurt just getting high.

Apparently he had what is known in some circles as a heroin metabolism. Charlie Parker had it; William S. Burroughs had it. It is a system that thrives on heroin, that can channel a normally strength-sapping drug into energy and creativity. "I was way more miserable during all the tours that I was vomiting every night and not eating and being totally straight," Kurt said to Azerrad. "I was way more of a bastard and a negative person. They couldn't be around me half the time. I was just looking straight ahead and concentrating on not puking all the time so that it was hard for anyone to communicate with me. But when I started doing drugs, I was feeling fine—and happy for the first time in a long time."

That spring, Nirvana had a dispute about publishing royalties that almost broke up the band. They had originally agreed on a three-way split, even though Kurt wrote ninety percent of the music. Now that *Nevermind* was so phenomenally successful, he decided he wanted more—and he wanted it to be retroactive to the release of *Nevermind*. "I realized how much more pressures are on me and how I deserve a little bit more because I'm the lead singer, all these perspectives are being written about me, I have to take all that pressure," he said, sounding as if he were reciting a litany.

For someone who had shown remarkably little ambition or image-consciousness up to this point, these are implausible words. They sound far more like the words of someone who had always been driven by ambition and image, and who was now interested in securing a giant slice of the Nirvana pie for her unborn daughter. Kurt eventually got his retroactive seventy-five percent of Nirvana's publishing royalties. Courtney got even less popular with his bandmates. Then they all went on tour together.

Nobody seemed to think Nirvana's European tour was a good idea, but nobody could stop its awful momentum—except Courtney. Experiencing mild contractions in Spain, she became terrified that she was about to miscarry. Kurt flew home with her. They arrived to find that a pipe in their bathroom had burst, drenching Kurt's favorite guitar and a bunch of his tapes and notebooks in black sludge. This plunged him into depression, and abandoning the methadone therapy he'd been on, he started shooting up again.

Hole was attracting the attention of major labels—including, to Courtney's chagrin, Madonna's Maverick. "Madonna's interest in me was kind of like Dracula's interest in his latest victim," she said later. After an intense bidding war, they ended up signing with Nirvana's label, Geffen, for $1 million. Courtney and Rosemary Carroll, her lawyer, demanded and got better contract terms than Nirvana. She was eight months pregnant. The baby was healthy. Kurt checked back into Cedars-Sinai Medical Center, swearing to give up drugs for good before his daughter was born.

Eric Erlandson kept watch over Courtney and Kurt during the twilight detox days of early August. "He totally saved our lives during that whole time," Kurt recalled in *Rolling Stone.* "He was the only piece of reality, the only calm person who was there as an example of what life could be like afterward, once this crazy shit was over."

They were still in pain, but they were excited about becoming parents and looking forward to a rich, creative future.

Then the September 1992 issue of *Vanity Fair* hit the stands, and everything changed forever.

CHAPTER FIFTEEN

◇

"I wouldn't have thought that I could be dwarfed or squashed or

raped or incredibly hurt by a story in that magazine," Courtney

said later. "But the power of it was so intense. It was unbelievable.

I read a fax of it and my bones shook. I knew that my world was

over. I was dead. That was it. The rest of my life. Not only was I

going to walk around with a big black mark, but any happiness

that I had known, I was going to have to fight for, for the rest of

my life. It shouldn't be that way, but I exposed myself to it. Had

I not taken drugs in the first place, I would have been lucid enough to know what she was about. I wouldn't have been candid. I would have figured out where I fit in the scheme of the *Vanity Fair* world."

"She" was Lynn Hirschberg, the author of a seven-thousand-word hatchet job entitled "Strange Love." She had interviewed Courtney over the course of several days in a chic restaurant, in a vintage clothing store, even in the couple's Fairfax apartment, which she described in lovingly squalid detail. She had gained Courtney's trust, slipped undetected through her bullshit monitor. She had written a completely humorless piece about a woman whose public persona consisted largely of sarcasm and hyperbole.

The article trotted out all of Courtney's demons: the ludicrous but persistent rumor that she had gotten Kurt hooked on heroin . . . the whispered suspicion that Hole had gotten their Geffen deal because she was married to Kurt . . . and, crucially, the fact that she had used heroin during the early stages of her pregnancy.

Hirschberg exerted herself to suggest that Courtney had done drugs long after she *knew* she was pregnant, was possibly still doing them. "Even the most tolerant industry insiders" reportedly expressed fear for the health of the child, and "one close friend" was quoted as saying, "We're all worried about that baby." (No one expressed any concern for Kurt, who *was* on drugs and had already begun to collect guns, unless you count the "someone close to [Nirvana]" who said, "Courtney always has a hidden agenda, and Kurt doesn't. He's definitely being led.")

Even Kat had joined in the slagfest. "Courtney's delusional," she was quoted as saying. "Last night, I had a dream that I killed her. I was really happy." (Hirschberg claimed that "none of this fazes Courtney," but a year later, the unfazed one was still repeating the lines "I dream she's dead and I wake up happy. She dreams I'm dead and she wakes up happy" in her notebook.)

The piece was sprinkled with factual errors, such as "[Kurt and Courtney] first met eight or so years ago" (it had been less than four) and "Reportedly, Kurt didn't do much more than drink until he met Courtney" (Kurt seldom drank because of his stomach problems, and his pre-Courtney use of opiates has been well documented). But no one noticed these small inconsistencies, because the overall portrait was too absorbing. Hirschberg described Courtney as "a train-wreck personality: she may be awful, but you can't take your eyes off her."

Then, of course, there was the picture. Michel Comte's infamous photograph showed Courtney heavily pregnant and disheveled in a black bra and a see-through bed-jacket, the first two fingers of her left hand half-curled in a characteristic smoker's gesture. She had, in fact, been smoking a cigarette during the photo shoot. *Vanity Fair* editor Tina Brown ordered it airbrushed out, but someone leaked the information, and soon magazines all over the world were bidding for the original photo.

Courtney and Kurt bought the entire roll for $25,000. Courtney wanted to sue Hirschberg and *Vanity Fair,* but was dissuaded by her lawyers, who were concerned that litigation would only serve to perpetuate the scandal.

Two weeks before the baby was due, Courtney joined her husband in Cedars-Sinai.

Kurt only dimly realized what was going on. Detoxing had almost killed him this time. While he lay there feeding off an IV tube, vomiting air, and begging for the occasional shot of morphine, gastrointestinal specialists swarmed around him, each hoping to discover the source of his mysterious pain. A patient with an unidentifiable malady was interesting; a *rich* patient with such a malady was positively captivating.

One day Kurt dragged himself to Courtney's room and sat on the end of her bed crying from the pain. He said he was breaking up the band, that they would leave town as soon as Frances was born. "Twenty years in the Dakota," he kept saying, referring to John and Yoko, "twenty years stuck inside the Dakota, I won't let that happen to you."

Courtney went into labor in the early hours of August 18, 1992. She hauled herself out of bed and wheeled her IV stand all the way to Kurt's wing of the hospital with an anxious battalion of doctors and nurses trailing along behind her. She yanked Kurt's covers off and screamed into his face, "You get out of this bed and you come down *now!* You are not leaving me to do this by myself, *fuck you!*"

Kurt dragged himself to the delivery room and made a valiant attempt to watch his daughter being born. "I'm having the baby, it's coming out, he's puking, he's passing out, and I'm holding his hand and rubbing his stomach while the baby's coming out of me," Courtney recalled. "It was pretty weird."

Frances Bean Cobain was born at 7:48 A.M. She weighed seven pounds, one ounce. "The infant is in good condition, is feeding well and growing at the normal rate expected for a new-born," a press release from Nirvana's management would announce a few days later. "The vicious rumors that Frances was suffering any withdrawals at the time of birth are completely false, and in fact, she has not suffered any discomfort since delivery."

That was true enough. But the press release didn't mention the discomfort her parents had suffered. Kurt had realized just what the *Vanity Fair* article could mean to his family, and he was hysterical over it. A social worker burst into Courtney's room waving a copy of *Vanity Fair* and vowing to take her baby away. Her own doctor, Michael Horwitz, seemed to take perverse pleasure in showing her an article from *The Globe*. ROCK STAR'S BABY IS BORN A JUNKIE, the tabloid trumpeted. Claiming that Frances had experienced "agonizing withdrawal . . . shivering, cramps, and muscle spasms," the article was accompanied by a gruesome photograph of a dead crack baby.

Courtney told *Rolling Stone* in late 1994,

> [Kurt] brought a gun to the hospital the day after our daughter was born. I was like, "I'll go first. I can't have you do it first. I go first." I held this thing in my hand and I felt that thing that they said in *Schindler's List:* I'm never going to know what happens to me. And what about Frances? Sort of rude. "Oh, your parents died the day after you were born."
>
> I just started talking him out of it. I said, "Fuck you, you can't chicken out. I'm gonna do it." But I made him give me the gun, and I had Eric take it away. I don't know what he did with it.

David Geffen sent them a congratulatory note, adding, "I know that you are upset about the recent article on Courtney and the attacks made on her character . . . The press have a way of sabotaging your privacy. The thing you have to remember is that these things pass and people quickly forget about articles of this type. You just have to let your life go on."

But no one would be allowed to forget about the *Vanity Fair* article anytime soon, least of all Courtney and Kurt. Courtney's attorney, Rosemary Carroll, believes the article led the Los Angeles County Department of Children's Services to begin action against the Cobains.

Children's Services went after the Cobains with a vengeance. The Cobains cooperated by going through a series of humiliating interviews and inspections, found doctors and other character witnesses to swear they were off drugs, even submitted financial statements to prove how well cared for their child would be. Nonetheless, when Frances Bean was two weeks old, Courtney and Kurt were forced to surrender custody of her to Courtney's half sister Jaimee.

For two months, Kurt and Courtney lived in the apartment next to Jaimee's while they fought to keep their daughter. They saw Frances every day, but they were never supposed to be alone with her. Courtney's song "I Think That I Would Die," with its refrain "Who took my baby" and the explosive line "It's not yours —FUCK YOU!" dates from this period.

The Cobains were finally allowed to take Frances home, but only on the condition that they submit to frequent urine tests and visits from a social worker. On September 22, Courtney's new doctor, Robert P. Fremont, M.D., wrote a letter stating, "Starting September 9th, 1992 [Courtney] has been given random urine tests which have all been entirely clean. She is seeing a drug counselor, a clinical psychologist, attending aftercare meetings at CPC Westwood and is examined in my office weekly. She seems determined to succeed and her prognosis is very good with the above safeguards in place."

L.A. seemed hostile now, wounded by the race riots of the spring, full of bad blood. "I *hate* L.A.," Kurt told *The Advocate*. "I love the weather, but I can't stand being there. A lot of it has to do with the responsibility of driving around with the baby in the car. People are so rude . . . I'm not that bad a driver, and I get in a wreck almost every day." They began making arrangements to buy a house in Seattle.

More hurts and disappointments were to come. In October, Julian Cope took out a full-page ad for his new single in selected outlets of the music press. The copy consisted of a long diatribe written by Julian, which declared, among other things, "Free Us (The Rock'n'Roll Fans) From Nancy Spungen–Fixated Heroin A-Holes Who Cling To Our Greatest Rock Groups And Suck Out Their Brains." He later told *Select* magazine, "She needs shooting and I'll shoot her."

Courtney's crime, of course, was becoming more famous than Julian.

"It hurt me so much," Courtney told *Q* magazine. "Yeah, I'm insane and crazy, but I didn't do anything inappropriate, weird, or bad. I don't understand why he did it. He's a really tolerant, lovely person who showed me a lot of compassion and gave me self-belief. He's lucid, not a madman or a druid, and I would've loved it if he'd liked my records. I just wanted him to be proud of me. I never exploited our relationship. It was incredibly stupid of him."

This looked good in *Q*, but her private fury was more eloquent. She wrote to Julian,

> Dear fucker,
>
> Imagine that it's 1983, 82 81 and 80, you're a teenage piece of white trash and not even remotely decorative, but you love the great rock dream and it's all you've got . . . And you buy a guitar and it burns like a coal in your hand and you feel some power and for once it isn't the power of being made fun of or picked on, it's the shallow mystic power of self-respect, the power to change the fucking world the way it is to you, the power to culturally uplift, in short, the power to save the world— THAT WHAT YOU THINK OF ME MAKES ME VIOLENTLY ILL, THAT YOU BELIEVE WHAT YOU'VE READ IN TWO ARTICLES, articles in magazines that apparently you've been waiting desperately for as opposed to say the dozens of "magazine" articles about me that have to do with my not so worthless work on this earth as an artist and for a brief moment the cultural peer of my fucking husband, that you despise Madonna but are

143

too much of a lemming and a mainstream IDIOT
to understand that my bona fide Nancy days only
began as a result of me laughing in her face and her
sending her toady/best friend to destroy me and try
to lock me up for 20 years in the Dakota . . .

Around the same time, the Cobains discovered a pair of English girls, Victoria Clarke and Britt Collins, sniffing around their hindquarters. Collins had little journalistic experience other than reviews for music zines. Clarke's claim to credibility was having dated Shane MacGowan from the Pogues, and she still used his name to talk her way in wherever she could.

They tried to convince a number of friends and industry insiders that their book project had Nirvana's blessing; Clarke even intimated that she had slept with Dave Grohl. They interviewed Falling James Moreland, from whom we have already heard. A neighbor reported seeing a woman of Clarke's description trying to break into the Cobains' house. It was obviously going to be another hatchet job. Kurt and Courtney panicked.

"If anything comes out in this book which hurts my wife, I'll fucking hurt you," said the first message on Victoria Clarke's answering machine (there were nine altogether, in two-minute increments). The voice was young, hoarse, tired, and bitter:

> I love to be fucked, I love to be blackmailed, I'll give
> you anything you want, I'm begging you. I'm on my
> knees and my mouth is wide open. You have absolutely
> no fucking idea what you're doing . . . you parasitic
> little cunts . . . at this point I don't give a flying fuck if
> I have this recorded that I'm threatening you. I suppose I could throw out a few hundred thousand dollars
> to have you snuffed out, but maybe I'll try it the legal
> way first.

Courtney, Krist, and Dave left messages too, all on the same drunken night, but Kurt's were the only ones Clarke released to *Select* magazine. According to sources who have heard the entire tape, the unreleased messages contained such cruel descriptions of Clarke and Collins that the would-be biographers were too embarrassed to make them public.

◇

CHAPTER SIXTEEN

As soon as possible, the Cobains returned to Seattle. Courtney felt that she never wanted to live in L.A. again, and Kurt had never wanted to live there at all. They bought a house in Carnation, twenty miles east of Seattle, and rented another in Sand Point, north of downtown Seattle on the shore of Lake Washington. The rented house, where they spent most of their time, had a spiral staircase and balconies that reminded them of New Orleans, a city they both loved. They got a chihuahua, but all three of them hated it so deeply and immediately that they gave it to the Mexican movers as a tip.

It was a creative time for them. The presence of Frances awed them, made them goofy with love for her and each other. They composed and sang songs for her ("Frances Bean, Frances Bean, the prettiest girl I've ever seen"). Kurt designed a "perpetual care chair" with toys and a self-feeding bottle. They filmed her un-spooling entire rolls of toilet paper with Kurt's help. They played with Frances constantly, thrilled by her reaction to every new stimulus. She became rather stoic as a result. They even took her to the MTV Video Music Awards, where Courtney nearly had to kick Axl Rose's ass.

Kurt later attempted to explain the MTV Awards episode to *The Advocate:*

> [Guns N' Roses] actually tried to beat us up. Courtney and I were in the eating area backstage, and Axl walked by. So Courtney yelled, "Axl! Axl, come over here!" We just wanted to say hi to him—we think he's a joke, but we just wanted to say something to him. So I said, "Will you be the godfather of our child?" I don't know what had happened before that to piss him off, but he took his aggressions out on us and began screaming bloody murder.
>
> These were his words: "You shut your bitch up, or I'm taking you down to the pavement!" Everyone around us just burst into tears of laughter. She wasn't even saying anything mean, you know? So I turned to Courtney and said, "Shut up, bitch!" And everyone laughed, and he left. So I guess I did what he wanted me to—be a man . . .
>
> Later, after we played our show and were walk-ing back to our trailer, the Guns N' Roses entourage

came walking toward us. They have at least fifty body-guards apiece: huge, gigantic, brain-dead oafs ready to kill for Axl at all times. They didn't see me, but they surrounded Krist, and Duff [McKagan of Guns N' Roses] wanted to beat Krist up, and the body-guards started pushing Krist around. He finally escaped, but throughout the rest of the evening, there was a big threat of either Guns N' Roses themselves or their goons beating us up. We had to hide out.

Since then, every time Axl has played a show he's said some comment about me and Courtney. When he was in Seattle, he said, "Nirvana would rather stay home and shoot drugs with their bitch wives than tour with us" . . . He is insane, though. I was scared. I couldn't possibly beat him up. I know he would beat me up if he had the chance.

In December 1992, the Cobains appeared on the cover of *Spin's* Year in Music issue. All three of them looked clean, fragile, and very beautiful. The exclusive interview inside, conducted by Sub Pop's Jonathan Poneman, was titled "Family Values." In the same issue, Nirvana was named Artist of the Year, and Axl Rose was roundly vilified. Kurt and Courtney seemed to have come through the fire.

"I've been writing a lot," Courtney said. "[Hole] should have an album out in about six months and then a tour. I haven't had a band in six months or so. It's sort of like having your arm cut off." The six-month deadline proved to be unrealistic, but she was eager to demonstrate how far back she had come.

She wasn't airbrushing herself, though. When Poneman asked whether pregnancy and motherhood had affected her artistic per-spective, though, she bristled at the idea. "What am I supposed to do, turn into fucking Mother Teresa all of a sudden? Am I supposed to write a country record because I had a baby? I've felt more sexual warfare, political, medical, and media terror in the last couple months than I've ever felt in my whole life."

But now, she believed, Frances was "guaranteed a one-hundred-percent perfect childhood. We knew we could give her what we didn't get—loyalty and compassion, encouragement. We knew we could give her a real home and spoil her rotten . . . I grew up living with my therapist and my stepbrother and my mother's ex-lover and on and on and I just think it sucks. This is just a personal preference. I think when you get married, it should be forever. Even though I did get married once and it was annulled. I don't know. For myself, I just want to have kids by the same person and stay with the same person."

Perhaps saying it would make it true. Perhaps Kurt hearing her say it would keep him alive. She was already afraid for him, had always been afraid for him: he was such a raw nerve, compelled to keep hurting and flaring and longing for succor. One day he'd found a Valentine candy box in which Courtney kept her old letters from Billy Corgan. Kurt hated Billy, partly because of Billy's obvious talent, mostly just because Billy had been first. Furious, he crawled into bed and scrawled out the lyrics to "Heart-Shaped Box" in ten minutes. The box that held Billy's letters appears in the "Heart-Shaped Box" video.

In January 1993, Nirvana played a disastrous show in Buenos Aires, Argentina. The opening act, Calamity Jane, was driven off the stage by shouted slurs *("Puta madre!")* and hurled objects. Incensed by the crowd's treatment of the all-female band, Nirvana deliberately screwed up their entire set.

It was the first time Kurt had been away since Frances was born, and Courtney sank into a stupor of depression. She faxed Kurt a note:

you've only been gone a day but today her turtle tooth came IN, I mean YOU CAN SEE IT, a little pearly girlrazor right where it's supposed to be, in the middle on the bottom, I was crying in the bath with her for nearly a half hour straight, and she kept looking up and grinning, looking up and rooting, and I'd sob and sob and feel so guilty to burden her, and she reached up and put her arms around me and comforted me! TOOK TIME OUT OF HER BUSY TEAR AND ROOT SCHEDULE! Queen Narcissus herself! . . .

In February, Kurt appeared on the cover of *The Advocate,* the oldest and most successful gay news magazine in the United States. In the interview, the reporter pegged Courtney (who left early on) as "tailor-made for media attention, blessed and cursed with what seems an almost genetic inability to censor herself."

Kurt wanted to make a good impression on gay readers, so the *Advocate* piece is one of his most thoughtful, least sarcastic interviews. He talked about the times he and Krist had spray-painted graffiti like HOMOSEXUAL SEX RULES and GOD IS GAY in Aberdeen. He commented on one of the scourges of his generation: "[We] are not going to put up with the same Reaganite bullshit we were subjected to when we were younger. I was helpless when I was twelve, when Reagan got elected, and there was nothing I could do about that. But now this generation is growing up, and they're in their mid-twenties; they're not putting up with it."

He more or less apologized for not having had any actual gay experiences by saying, "I'm definitely gay in spirit and I probably could be bisexual. But I'm married, and I'm more attracted to Courtney than I ever have been toward a person, so

151

there's no point in my trying to sow my oats at this point.[1] If I wouldn't have found Courtney, I probably would have carried on with a bisexual lifestyle. But I just find her totally attractive in all ways."

He also said, in the course of discussing the impact of the *Vanity Fair* article and other negative press, "Courtney's had misconceptions about herself all her life. I talk to people who knew Courtney five years ago, and she was way more of a volatile, fucked-up person than she is now. She was insane at times. People would see her at parties just begging for attention. I never could have predicted a successful marriage with this person a few years ago. It just couldn't have happened."

Of course, life was never perfect. In Seattle, Courtney saw a lot more of the Olympia love-rockers she'd always hated. The Seattle-Olympia contingent was dominated partly by Riot Grrrl bands like Bikini Kill and partly by "Calvinists," followers of K Records' Calvin Johnson, who espoused clean living and childlike joy in life. Everything was pastel, P.C., and fuzzy-cute. For instance, one of the Olympians' favorite ways to spend an evening was to organize a rousing cakewalk. Everyone would make a cake and put a silly label on it, like "Cake with the most boyfriends," "Cake with the least boyfriends," "Ugliest cake," "Prettiest cake." Then, just like at your second-grade school fair, they would parade around a circle of numbers until the music stopped and someone won a cake. "*I* have the most cake of anyone in this town," Courtney decided, and proceeded to pen a line that would follow her forever.

One annoyance was Tobi Vail, Bikini Kill's drummer and Kurt's ex-girlfriend. Tobi had started writing to Kurt while

---

[1] Courtney later insinuated that Kurt had, in fact, sown a few oats with Michael Stipe of R.E.M. Stipe, a good friend of the couple, commented, "I just have to laugh. It's very much in that rock'n'roll mythology. The baby and the nanny were with us the whole time. What a night of sexual escapades that would have sounded like if that had been mentioned."

Courtney was pregnant. At Kurt's request, Courtney screened the letters and wrote back:

> . . . You are writing lipstick-smeared half psycho con-trived love letters to my husband and the father of my 6 month old fetus/daughter. It's so sick, one time it's an eternal love letter, one time it's a let's be friends letter, one time it's a letter to me and then it's these missives of secret messages, the common thread being this non-stop desperation to RECORD WITH my husband while I sit here lactating and the answer is no, no, no, no, and at least I read your letters and am responding, Kurt barely made it through 2 pages, I had to pick out the sexy highlights.

Tobi had backed off then. But now she was around again, and Courtney hated seeing her. Another irritant was Calvin Johnson. In 1989 and 1990, K Records released an EP and two singles by a band who called themselves Courtney Love. One of its members, Lois Maffeo, had somehow acquired one of Courtney's diaries and given it to Calvin, who reportedly still keeps it locked in a desk drawer.

Courtney called him and told him the band needed to change its name. "Calvin, people are buying Courtney Love records thinking it's me, and I would never say 'I lost my head on about a million dates'—it's quite embarrassing."

"Lady"—he always addressed her by this sarcastic title—"lady, no one knows who you are!" Then he hung up on her.

She saw him soon afterward at a Fugazi show, helping the hardcore band load their equipment. "Calvin," she said, coming up behind him, "are you gonna stop putting out those records, or am I gonna kick you in the butt?"

"Shut up!" he snapped, and unwisely turned his back on her. Courtney swung her high-heeled foot and caught him square in the crack. He must have felt it, because K didn't put out any more Courtney Love records, and Lois Maffeo eventually changed her band's name to "Lois." Nonetheless, Courtney noted in her journal, "Lois, I'll probably punch you if I see you: I don't like people making money off my name and lying about it.[2] I believe in punching."

To send up the Riot Grrrls and Calvinists, Courtney, Kurt, and Patty Schemel started a fake band called Nighty Nite. "We pretended we were two sisters from Marysville, seventeen and sixteen, Dottie and Clara. We put the pitch way up on the four-track and we made up these really stupid songs like 'Lemonade Nation' and 'Twister' and 'Hello Kitty,' just crap like that. Sent the tapes out to all the appropriate people: *Maximumrocknroll,* Kim and Thurston, Bikini Kill, Fugazi, Calvin, Slim Moon. Huge buzz. 'We want a lemonade nation revolution and we want it now!' "

It wasn't easy going out in Seattle, either. Kurt got recognized everywhere, and there was always some bozo ready to fuck with the big rock star just to see what he'd do. If Courtney was with him, she'd give the bozo an eloquent cussing-out, which embarrassed Kurt even more. And he was still obsessing about bad press and the effect it could have on his family. "I used to be a funny person, always going out of my way to look on the funnier side of life, but I've withdrawn back into a bad attitude," he told Michael Azerrad. "I'm sure it will just be a matter of time because the positive things—the baby and the wife—are so great, they're so etched into my life as being positive things that I'm blessed with and grateful for, that if people just keep their fucking mouths shut and stop the accusations, I'll probably be okay. But I just don't see it ending. Just yesterday, another fucking article came out . . ."

---

[2] Lois claimed that she and Courtney had once been roommates and had simultaneously conceived of "Courtney Love" as the perfect name for a rock star.

Hurtful as they might be, the articles were not entirely without foundation. Kurt had started making trips down to Capitol Hill, Seattle's prime zone for scoring heroin. Courtney gave in to temptation only a couple of times. Kurt, though, began to develop his worst and final habit.

On March 23, 1993, all charges against the Cobains were formally dropped by the Department of Children's Services in L.A. Kurt and Courtney already had legal custody of Frances; this meant that they would no longer have to endure visits from social workers or pass urine tests.

That spring, Hole played a women-only festival in London organized by English Riot Grrrl band Huggy Bear. (Eric was admitted as an honorary woman.) Courtney had mixed feelings about the sexual separatism, but admitted that it was wonderful to be able to crowd-surf in trust rather than fear of digital rape and possible injury.

Even so, she couldn't avoid getting into a shouting match with members of the audience—she committed the cardinal (in this crowd) sin of referring to a woman journalist as "fat." Just before Hole went onstage, someone mentioned to Courtney that Linda Duff from the *Daily Star* was in the house. As Courtney understood it, Ms. Duff had been responsible for printing the photo of the dead crack baby that was supposed to be Frances Bean. Courtney had been slugging down vodka-and-grapefruit juice, and she grabbed the mike and roared, "There's a woman here called Linda Duff from the *Daily Star* and she's blonde and she's fat and I WANT HER GONE!"

"You have no *right* to call her fat," came an immediate catcall from the audience.

Hole launched into their first song without responding. But before the song was over, Courtney had decided to apologize. After all, fat was a feminist issue, and there was no need to alienate a whole clubful of women just to skewer one more parasite. Unfortunately, the apology didn't come out very well. "I'm sorry I called her fat. Maybe having people call her that has made her into the twisted and bitter person she obviously is."

The same catcaller spoke up. *"An apology's not enough! You shouldn't have said it in the first place!"*

Courtney rolled her eyes. It was no use. "LOOK," she yelled, "I'M NOT POLITICALLY CORRECT AND I'M NOT THE VOICE OF A GENERATION, SO <u>FUCK YOU</u>!!!"

The crowd cheered, and Courtney hoisted her guitar proudly.

Meanwhile, Nirvana was in Minnesota recording *In Utero* with producer Steve Albini. Though she had listed his band Big Black as an early influence, Courtney soon decided Albini was a misogynist of the lowest order. He called her a "psycho hosebeast" in print, and she responded with uncharacteristic (if pointed) restraint, "The only way Steve Albini would think I was a perfect girlfriend would be if I was from the East Coast, played the cello, had big tits and small hoop earrings, wore black turtlenecks, had all matching luggage, and never said a *word.*"

Hole was ready to record an album too, but they still didn't have a bass player. They asked Kristen Pfaff again, and this time she said yes.

◇

CHAPTER SEVENTEEN

Courtney was ready to get to work. She found Kurt's renewed

habit distracting, infuriating, and sometimes terrifying.

In May, he came home just as he was beginning to overdose

and had to be sent to Harborview Medical Center. In June,

Courtney called police to the house. The police report stated,

"Suspect Kurt Cobain and victim Courtney Love had gotten into

an argument over guns in the household. Victim Courtney stated

that she threw a glass of juice into suspect Kurt's face and that suspect Kurt pushed her in turn. Victim pushed suspect back, at which time suspect pushed victim to floor and began choking her, leaving a scratch."

They hauled Kurt off to jail in his bathrobe. He spent three hours there before being released on $950 bail, which Courtney paid. She refused to press charges, of course; she had only hoped that the police might take the guns away, but they hadn't. Kurt kept buying pistols, shotguns, even an M16. The presence of a gun or two had once felt comforting, a barrier against the rest of the world. Now, through Kurt's obsession, through Courtney's fear for Frances and her own cold fascination with such easy instruments of death, the guns were separating them.

Hole's new lineup was her salvation. Patty Schemel was proving herself to be one of the best drummers in rock'n'roll. Eric and Kristen Pfaff had fallen in love, and their chemistry added to the intensity of the music, especially live. They had more than enough material to make a good record, and they booked studio time for the fall.

In July, Hole played a blazing set at Seattle's Off-Ramp. Then they left for a tour of Europe. Courtney was a little apprehensive about leaving Frances with Kurt, but he had the nanny to help him, and he had sworn to be a good daddy. She thought the responsibility might force him to do so in a way he never could when she was around.

Kurt and Frances had a fine time, but his idea of being a good daddy didn't preclude heroin use. If he'd tried to kick during Courtney's absence, he'd have been sick, miserable, and useless. This way, he felt fine. Frances was only a year old, he rationalized, too young to know or care if he was high.

Hole came back from Europe and flew to Atlanta to begin recording *Live Through This* at Triclops Studio, the same place Smashing Pumpkins had made *Siamese Dream*. Courtney knew this was going to be their breakthrough album. Geffen would be throwing all their publicity muscle behind it. She had twelve strong tracks, musicians she loved, and complete creative control. She selected the photographer, model, and stylist for the beauty-queen cover art. And she provided the back cover photo of herself at age eight, stringy-haired and barefoot, dressed in her cast-off hippie clothes.

Meanwhile, *In Utero* debuted at number one on the *Billboard* charts. While Courtney was in the studio, Frances accompanied her father on Nirvana's first American tour in two years. The addition of ex-Germs guitarist Pat Smear allowed Kurt to concentrate more fully on singing. He had detoxed before the tour, and his stomach pain didn't flare up right away as it always had before.

"I needed time to collect my thoughts and readjust," he told *Rolling Stone*, explaining why Nirvana had stayed off the road so long. "[Success] hit me so hard, and I was under the impression that I didn't really need to go on tour, because I was making a whole bunch of money. Millions of dollars. Eight million to ten million records sold—that sounded like a lot of money to me."

Unfortunately, Kurt had had no idea how rock finances work, and now his family needed the cash infusion that a Nirvana tour could bring. Because his stomach wasn't hurting him, he was actually able to enjoy some of this tour. One night he was able to eat an entire pizza, something he hadn't done in years. The simple pleasures of a full stomach and his daughter's company were better than drugs, at least for now.

Hole played a show in Atlanta on Halloween night. "All these weird purists showed up," Courtney told *Rolling Stone*. "Total fans, but every time we'd go into one of our pop songs, they'd start chanting: 'Don't do it! Sellout!' I heard one girl saying to this other girl, 'They *used* to be so much better.' So I just started talking to the audience. I said, 'I've grown, you haven't, the sex really isn't good anymore, and you know what? There's always gonna be a shitty band with girls in it that can't play.' Girls were throwing Riot Grrrl zines at me and stuff. I was like, 'Uh, I'm really glad you're here, girls, but check it out: I can write a bridge now.' "

Toward the end of Nirvana's tour, while *Live Through This* was being mixed, Courtney flew to meet Kurt before embarking on Hole's tour with the Lemonheads. While on board the tour bus, she conducted a *Rolling Stone* interview by cellular phone with Kurt listening (and occasionally commenting) in the background. The interview reflects her determination at the time to put her life in order and gain perspective from the things that had caused her pain.

What was the Walt Whitman quote about when you die, leaving a fertile patch of grass and a happy child? When you're dying and your life is flashing before your eyes, I don't think you're gonna be thinking about how much you hate some journalist. You're gonna be thinking about the great things that you did, the horrible things that you did, the emotional impact that someone had on you and that you had on somebody else. Those are the things that are relevant. To have some sort of emotional impact that transcends your time, that's great. As long as you don't mess it up by being undignified when you're old.

I hope that I'll be dignified. I *know* I won't be pathetically addicted to any kind of bullshit. I'd like to have a really large brood of children and a good garden, and I'd like to grow really great hybrid roses and have a lot of dogs and a lot of cats and get *Victoria* magazine and have a goddamn nice house! I don't think I want to be sitting on a porch drinking whiskey and singing the blues. Knowing me, I'd probably end

up at a bar, asking some guy to get me a martini. Still
bleaching my hair at fifty-nine.

Nirvana finished their tour with an appearance on MTV's
acoustic rock show *Unplugged,* recorded in New York on November 18. They were joined on the candlelit stage by cellist Lori
Goldston, and Cris and Curt Kirkwood of the Meat Puppets
stopped in to guest on three numbers from their seminal *Meat
Puppets II* album. Nearly half the songs in the set were covers,
and Kurt's voice carried the show; that night it seemed as if he
could wring even more raw emotion out of other people's words
than he could from his own.

Heard now, the performance is like a blueprint of his future.
"I don't have to think / I only have to do it," he half-whispers on
the Meat Puppets' "Oh Me." "Don't expect me to cry for all the
reasons you had to die," he warns (himself?) on the Vaselines'
"Jesus Doesn't Want Me for a Sunbeam." Eeriest is his version of
David Bowie's "The Man Who Sold the World," a ghostly song
to begin with. Though most of the audience wasn't aware of it,
Kurt put his own twist on the original lyrics: "I gazed a gazeless
stare / With multimillionaires / I must have died alone / A long,
long time ago . . ."

And, of course, there are several of his own saddest lines:

"And I swear that I don't have a gun . . ."

"It's okay to eat fish, cause they don't have any feelings."[1]

"I think I'm dumb / Or maybe just happy."

While Courtney was on the road, Nirvana received a plum
offer to headline Lollapalooza 1994. Dave and Krist wanted to
do it. Kurt didn't; in fact, he didn't even want to do the European
tour Nirvana already had scheduled for early 1994. Courtney
wanted him to skip the tour and do Lollapalooza. She faxed him

---

[1] This from a Pisces.

161

a three-page letter to state her case, which included dire predic-
tions of how Smashing Pumpkins would headline the festival if
Nirvana turned it down. (Kurt was still terribly jealous of Billy
Corgan.)

Nirvana finally committed to Lollapalooza. But Kurt just
didn't care anymore. His fire was gone, or he convinced himself
that it was. His stomach ailment had come back, and with it, a
crushing depression. He'd allowed himself to believe he might
finally be better. Now he knew he would never escape the pain he
had described to Michael Azerrad as "burning, nauseous, like the
worst stomach flu you can imagine. You can feel it throbbing like
you have a heart in your stomach . . . I can just feel it being all
raw and red."

He'd started taking Klonopin, a tranquilizer often prescribed
to artists for anxiety. And he had started using heroin again. The
combination made him intensely paranoid and caused him to
have hours-long blackouts.

In the midst of all this, the Cobains were house-hunting. On
January 19, 1994, they paid $1,485,000 for a property on Lake
Washington in Seattle's Madrona district. Fronted and flanked by
tall rhododendron hedges, the gray-shingled quarrystone mansion had been built by the Blaine family, who were among the
founders of Seattle, in 1901. A bower of wisteria arched over the
front door, and inside a formal staircase curved gracefully up to
the second floor. The largest of the five bedrooms had a huge
picture window overlooking the park across the road, the shim-
mering lake beyond, and the faraway veiled peaks of the Cas-
cades. The house was within easy reach of Capitol Hill, the
neighborhood where Kurt usually got his drugs.

There was a second building on the property, originally a
carriage house, now a garage with a small apartment above it,
that also looked out on the lake. Courtney would soon have the
apartment converted into a greenhouse for orchids.

At the beginning of February, against all his wishes, Kurt boarded a plane to Europe to begin Nirvana's European tour. Courtney stayed home to do publicity for *Live Through This*, which was scheduled for an April release and had already received advance praise from *Spin*, *Rolling Stone*, *The Advocate*, even *Newsweek*.

Nirvana's management had promised the band an easy schedule in Europe; instead they were booked for thirty-eight shows in twelve countries, a grueling itinerary that would keep them on the road more than two months. By February 16, Kurt's voice had begun to go, and he was already physically and mentally exhausted. "I was doing my thing with my band for the first time since forever," Courtney told *Rolling Stone*. "He was in Madrid, and he'd walked through the audience. The kids were smoking heroin off tinfoil, and the kids were going, 'Kurt! Smack!' and giving him the thumbs-up. He called me, crying . . . He did not want to become a junkie icon."

But he did want to do heroin. In Paris, he found some. Photographer Youri Lenquette captured Kurt, while high, putting the barrel of a gun in his mouth and pretending to fire it, his head jerking from the imaginary impact. Courtney was now in London doing interviews, and when Kurt found out Smashing Pumpkins were in London too, he became suspicious.

On the first of March, in Munich, his voice went out completely. He was diagnosed with severe laryngitis and bronchitis, and the remaining twenty-three shows were postponed. Kurt flew to Rome and checked into the Excelsior Hotel. Courtney joined him the next day, along with Frances and her nanny, Jackie. The couple had been apart for twenty-six days, a record.

Kurt had gone all out for Courtney when she got there. He'd bought her roses, champagne, even a piece of the Colosseum in tribute to her love of Roman history. They drank the champagne and began kissing, but somewhere along the way Courtney had had a Valium, and she fell asleep.

Courtney spoke to various media afterward:

> It was just horrible. He had those pills [Rohypnol] . . .
> He'd been in Slovenia or one of those gross places
> and I mean, he never drinks. He'd been on painkillers
> already and something for flu. He just thinks he's
> immortal . . .
>
> I turned over about three or four in the morning to
> make love, and he was gone. He was at the end of the
> bed with a thousand dollars in his pocket and a note
> saying, "You don't love me anymore. I'd rather die than
> go through a divorce." It was all in his head. I'd been
> away from him during our relationship maybe sixty
> days. *Ever.* I needed to be on tour. I had to do my
> thing . . . Goddamn, man. Even if I wasn't in the
> mood, I should have just laid there for him. All he
> needed was to get laid. He would have been fine . . .
>
> When the ambulance came for him I beat up a
> paparazzi. We were at the American Hospital and this
> guy starts interfering with Kurt's oxygen and he hit me
> in the jaw. So I hit him with all my force in his nuts.
>
> Kurt was in a coma for twenty hours and I was
> hysterical throughout. I mean, they had two tubes in
> his nose and two in his mouth, things coming out of
> every available artery . . . They had to put the glucose
> in through his neck. All of his life functions, including
> pissing, were being done by a machine.
>
> I mean, I have seen him get really fucked up before,
> but I have never seen him nearly eat it.

Kurt had used most of the champagne to wash down fifty
tablets of Rohypnol—not an easy task, since each pill came in its
own foil packet and had to be individually unwrapped. A strong
tranquilizer sometimes used to treat heroin withdrawal, Rohypnol

has become infamous in the United States (where it is legally unavailable) as "the date-rape pill." It dissolves easily in a drink, leaving no aftertaste, and when combined with alcohol it can knock someone out for hours.

Kurt was comatose when he arrived at Umberto I Polyclinic Hospital. His stomach was pumped and his vital signs stabilized; then he was transferred to the American Hospital outside Rome. For the next twenty hours, a media-driven feeding frenzy ensued. Was Kurt really dead? Was he brain-damaged? Had it been a suicide attempt? Had there been a note? No one knew much of anything, but everyone was willing to speculate.

Courtney was there when he opened his eyes. He couldn't talk, so she handed him a pencil and pad. Kurt wrote, "FUCK YOU," then, "Get these fucking tubes out of my nose."

"You're so silly," she whispered to him later, snuggled beside him in the hospital bed when the doctors and nurses had finished swarming around. "I'd never divorce you. You're crazy."

Kurt had just had a catheter removed, and getting a hard-on was painful for him, but they made love anyway. They had to. They'd almost lost the chance forever.

"He's not going to get away from me that easily," Courtney said soon afterward. "I'll follow him through hell." And she was about to.

◇

Conversation overheard on a flight from Rome to Seattle, March

12, 1994:

"Give me a Rohypnol."

"They're gone."

A silence. Five minutes later: "C'mon, give me a Rohypnol."

"They're *gone,* Kurt. They are gone. I dumped them all down

the fuckin' toilet. It's over."

"Fuck you, you lying bitch, give me a Rohypnol . . . Please . . ."

When they got home, Courtney banned heroin use in the house. Kurt could do it if he wanted to, she told him, but he had to go to a hotel. He went to a hotel. After two nights of this, Courtney was so insanely worried that she forbade him to do heroin anywhere *but* the house.

As well as heroin and Klonopin, Kurt had started doing a lot of speed. Never a big bather, he stopped washing altogether. He didn't sleep for a week. He seemed to have gone completely over the edge of madness; nothing he did made any sense. He dressed in hunting gear—boots, a heavy jacket, a cap with earflaps—and roamed around the house with a shotgun. Courtney contemplated grinding up Valium and feeding it to him in a drink just so his body could get some rest. Eventually he nodded off on his own.

On March 18, Courtney called 911 again. Kurt had locked himself in the bathroom with a bunch of guns, and Courtney was sure he was going to kill himself. Kurt managed to convince the cops that he wasn't suicidal and that he was in the bathroom hiding from Courtney, who had been trying to beat him up. He showed scratch marks on his back as proof.

The police confiscated four guns, twenty-five boxes of ammunition, and a bottle of pills. When the cops asked Kurt if he wanted to go someplace else, Kurt answered, "Anywhere but here." He got them to drop him off downtown, scored some drugs, and went up to the property in Carnation, where he spent the rest of the weekend alone.

One day Kurt found a stash of fan mail and magazines that Courtney had hidden—all filled with references to his drug addiction and the danger he was in. "If you die," a ten-year-old boy had written to him, "how do I go on?" They got into a physical fight over the papers, Courtney trying to tear them away, Kurt ripping out pages on the floor. "It's a cloud!" she sobbed. "It'll pass!"

"Damn right it'll pass; I'm not gonna make any fucking music ever again. I'm not gonna fucking be here to see it pass."

On March 25, in utter desperation, Courtney staged what is known in drug-counseling circles as an intervention. Krist Novoselic, Pat Smear, Kurt's old friend Dylan Carlson, and three of Nirvana's managers came to the house and took turns talking to him for five hours. They all threatened to abandon him, to fire him, to leave him to choose between life and death. Kurt sat through it with his eyes open, but nobody could tell if he heard them.

When the session was over, Courtney could see that it hadn't worked. Kurt had only been waiting for them to shut up so he could go take drugs. At that point she knew that, barring a miracle, her husband was going to kill himself.

At last she convinced him to enter the Exodus Center, a detox clinic in Marina del Rey, California, where he had been before. They agreed to send an ambulance for Kurt, but when it arrived, Kurt refused to get in. The attendants wrestled him out of the house. Courtney followed them outside and saw Kurt surrounded by people, spitting in any face that came near his, screaming at the top of his still-formidable lungs, "FUCK YOU!!! FUCK YOU!!! FUCK YOU!!!"

One of the attendants from Exodus pulled Courtney aside. "Legally, we can't force him to go," he told her. "If you love your husband, *you'll* go to L.A., and he'll follow you there."

Courtney saw that there was a car waiting for her. The managers flocked around her, tried to pull her into the car. She saw the top of Kurt's blonde head whipping furiously back and forth. She didn't want to go, but she knew she couldn't stay here anymore, not right now. Maybe these people knew what they were talking about, and Kurt would follow her to L.A.

"Goodbye," she called out to Kurt as she slipped into the car, but she didn't think he heard her.

Geffen's release of *Live Through This* was just two weeks away.

Courtney checked into the Peninsula Beverly Hills hotel, installing Frances and Jackie in an adjacent suite. Kurt called several times over the next few days. It was all Courtney could do not to fly home at once, but the intervention people insisted that she mustn't. Kurt would nod off on the phone, then become lucid and say, "Yeah, I'm gonna come check in." Instead, he wandered around Seattle for several days, turning up at Linda's Tavern, Ohm's comic-book shop, his drug dealer's house, looking sick, hollow, ghastly. The *Los Angeles Times* reported that Nirvana had pulled out of Lollapalooza, which was the first Courtney had heard of it. Amazingly, she didn't go ballistic; she knew that whatever happened now, Kurt would probably never tour again.

On March 30, Kurt and Dylan Carlson went to Stan Baker Sports and bought a Remington M11 twenty-gauge shotgun. Dylan signed for the purchase, paying $308.87 in cash. Despite the fact that he had been present at the intervention, Dylan Carlson says he had no idea Kurt was suicidal, and believed him when he said he wanted the gun for protection.

Kurt went home and stashed his prize. While he was at the house, Courtney called, and this time she persuaded him to come to L.A. Perhaps it was easier for him to go knowing he had the gun to come back to.

When Kurt arrived at Exodus, Courtney was forbidden to visit him for three days. "It wouldn't be healthy for your relationship," his counselor told her. Courtney was in agony because she couldn't see Kurt, and it appeared to her that she was being blamed (again) for his addiction. She was too desperate to fight their opinions; she just wanted them to make Kurt better. "I was actually listening to the grown-ups," she says.

On April 1, the nanny brought Frances to visit her father. He played with her for a little while, then saw them off and called Courtney from the pay phone in the hall. "No matter what happens," he told her, "I want you to know you made a really good record."

"Well . . . what do you mean?"

"Just remember, no matter what, I love you." He hung up. A few hours later, he went out to smoke a cigarette and climbed over the wall at the rear of the hospital grounds. Then he made his way to LAX, bought a ticket with his American Express card, and flew back to Seattle.

When Courtney found out Kurt had jumped the fence, she assumed he was still in L.A. She canceled his credit card, thinking he would call her when his money ran out. She went on a telephone crusade, calling rock stars to get drug dealers' numbers, calling drug dealers, driving around to their houses to satisfy herself that Kurt wasn't there.

In Seattle, Kurt went straight home. On the morning of April 2, he spoke briefly to Frances' former nanny, Michael "Cali" Dewitt, a guest in the house. Cali later told investigators that Kurt had looked sick but hadn't said anything overly strange.

After seeing Cali, Kurt took a cab downtown to purchase twenty-five shotgun cartridges at Seattle Guns. At 8:40 A.M., he tried to call Courtney but was blocked by the hotel switchboard, even though she had told them to hold all calls *except* those from her husband.

Kurt's last few days are a mystery, filled with conflicting stories and apocryphal sightings, unlikely claims and too-strenuous denials.

On April 5, he returned to the now-deserted house. He took Chim-Chim and hid the tiny plastic monkey in a secret spot, where Courtney would find it months later. He left the TV on. He retrieved the shotgun and climbed the nine weathered wooden steps to the greenhouse above the garage, where he locked one set of French doors and wedged a stool beneath the knobs of the other.

Looking out over dreary Lake Washington, Kurt smoked six cigarettes, drank some root beer, and scratched out a note to "Boddah," an invisible friend from his childhood. Then he injected a triple dose of heroin, and before it could incapacitate him, he took the shotgun's barrel into his mouth and pulled the trigger.

The noise was shattering, but the silence was endless.

Over the next two days, guests, workmen, and delivery people entered and left the house and grounds. No one looked in the greenhouse; there was no reason to, since you couldn't see into it from below. Night came in and shrouded the ruin; daylight glistened upon its cooling surfaces.

On the morning of April 7, Courtney was arrested at the Beverly Hills Peninsula. She called downstairs and asked for a dose of Benadryl, sleepily blurting out that she thought she might be having an allergic reaction to a new prescription. The desk clerk sent up a security guard. Upon judging Courtney to be "agitated," the rent-a-cop called paramedics and police. Courtney was certainly agitated: "What the fuck are you doing? Where's my Benadryl?" She became even more agitated when several policemen burst into the room and started ransacking her belongings. It seemed to her that more than one piece of jewelry disappeared during the search.

The officer in charge was a Detective Butkis. He reported that they had searched Courtney's "vomit and blood-spattered room" and found a syringe, a prescription pad, and a small, fancily wrapped packet containing a substance they believed to be heroin. (This turned out to be *vibbhuti*, Hindu good-luck ashes given to Courtney by Rosemary Carroll.) Butkis charged her with being "inebriated in the city of Beverly Hills" and took her to Century City Hospital, where a doctor said she was not high.

Nonetheless, when David Geffen learned of the incident, he called Courtney and urged her to check into rehab. She acquiesced in his wishes; maybe everyone would leave her the fuck alone there. And maybe Kurt would turn up. But she was terribly afraid for him. She and Kurt had always shared the same dreams

172

—not detail for detail, but interwoven somehow. But for the last two nights, Courtney hadn't had any dreams.

She woke up in Exodus on April 8 and turned on the TV to the hospital channel, a tape loop of soaring birds, crashing surf, and other soothing images set to new-age music. She was about to flip through the channels when Rosemary Carroll came in. Rosemary immediately glanced at the TV, then looked at her. From that gesture, and from Rosemary's face, Courtney knew.

She thought Kurt had been found dead from an overdose. Despite the guns, she had *always* thought that was what would happen.

"How?" she said, just to make sure, and Rosemary told her.

◇

She lay in the blood and stared up at the sky and wanted to fall

into it forever. *Are you there, are you there, are you fucking any-*

where? Are you an angel now? Fuck you . . .

Her counselor at Exodus had tried to prevent her from leav-

ing, but it was like getting in the way of an earthquake. They'd

taken a Lear jet back to Seattle, Courtney and Frances and Rose-

mary and Jackie the nanny, and had huddled in the backseat of a

limousine on the twenty-minute ride from Sea-Tac Airport to

175

the house. Kurt's body had been taken out that morning, a couple of hours after the electrician found him, and someone had picked up the detritus of his skull. But no one had cleaned up the blood. Courtney forbade anyone to do so.

She climbed the stairs to the greenhouse, probably with more fear than Kurt had, and stood in the doorway. The blood was an enormous Rorschach blot in which she could see all the loneliness ahead of her in the world, and all that Kurt had felt that she hadn't been able to get through. She knelt and put her hands in it. Then she stretched out in Kurt's blood, seeing what he had not seen, the creeping-in of night and the chill blue of dawn, the rain speckling the skylights, the callous sun. Sometimes she slept, sometimes she sang. And always, always, she searched for him and could not feel him.

The thought of Frances got her up off the floor. She searched the room for any trace of Kurt, and found a single, filthy scrap of hair held together by a tatter of scalp. She took it into the house and washed it, and washed herself as much as she could bear to. Then she put on one of Kurt's sweaters, crawled into bed and swallowed any drug that anyone brought her.

She got quite a lot. An endless stream of people flowed in and out of the bedroom, consoling, gawking, stealing things. She surrounded herself with people she trusted—Kat Bjelland, Wendy O'Connor, Dean Matthiesen. Nevertheless, almost all of Kurt's sweaters disappeared over the next few days. She discovered later that two reporters from a national magazine had been found in the bedroom trying to get her to talk.

Courtney remembered very little of it. Jackie brought Frances in, but the twenty-month-old was too little to comprehend what was going on. She only knew it was something exciting, like a birthday or Christmas. She didn't understand why her mother couldn't stop crying.

At one point, Courtney went to view Kurt's body. His eyes were sewn shut. The hardest thing to part with was his hands.

She had always thought they were so beautiful, and they had taught her so much: had guided hers on the guitar strings, had groped wildly for her in the dead of night, had bruised her. His hands were still beautiful. Courtney had plaster casts made.

Kurt's body was cremated later that day.

Courtney made a tape to be played at Kurt's public memorial service, held on April 10 at the Seattle Center, in a park near the Space Needle. Seven thousand fans gathered on the gray Sunday afternoon, most of them very young and utterly traumatized: sobbing, chanting, carving Kurt's name into their flesh.

"I don't really know what to say," Courtney's shattered voice told them. "I feel the same way you guys do. If you guys don't think that when I used to sit in this room when he played guitar and sing and feel so honored to be near him, you're crazy.

"Anyway, he left a note. It's more like a letter to the fucking editor. I don't know what happened. I mean, it was gonna happen. But it could have happened when he was forty. He always said he was going to outlive everybody and live to be a hundred and twenty.

"I'm not going to read you all the note, because it's none of the rest of your fucking business. But some of it is to you. I don't think it takes away from his dignity to read this, considering that it's addressed to most of you." Her voice was ragged, hollow. She took a deep breath. "He's such an asshole. I want you all to say 'Asshole' really loud."

The crowd obeyed.

She began to read Kurt's words. " 'This note should be pretty easy to understand. All the wording's from the Punk Rock 101. Over the years, it's my first introduction to the shall we say ethics involved with independence, and the embracement of your community has proven to be very true. I haven't felt the excitement of listening to as well as creating music, along with really writing something for two years now. I feel guilty beyond words about these things. For example, when we're backstage and the

177

lights go out and the manic roar of the crowd begins, it doesn't affect me the way in which it did for Freddie Mercury—' "

Courtney laughed, partly at Kurt's choice of stars, partly at a hazy memory of being at a party in Liverpool and going to wake Robin because Freddie Mercury had shown up.

" '—who seemed to love and relish the love and admiration from the crowd'—Well, Kurt, then so fucking what? Then don't be a rock star, you asshole—'which is something I totally admire and envy. The fact is, I can't fool you, any one of you. It simply isn't fair to you or to me. The worst crime I can think of would be to pull people off by faking it, pretending as if I'm having 100 percent fun.'

"No, Kurt, the worst crime I can think of is for you to just continue being a rock star when you fucking hate it. Just fucking stop.

" 'Sometimes I feel as if I should punch a time clock before I walk out onstage. I've tried everything within my power to appreciate it, and I do. God, believe me, I do. But it's not enough. I appreciate the fact that I and we have affected and entertained a lot of people. I must be one of those narcissists' "—Courtney gave another laugh, shorter and more bitter—" 'who only appreciate things when they're alone. I'm too sensitive.'

"*Awww.*

" 'I need to be slightly numb in order to regain the enthusiasm I once had as a child. On our last three tours I've had a much better appreciation for all the people I've known personally and as fans of our music. But I still can't get over the frustration, the guilt, and the empathy I have for everyone.' " Courtney's voice wavered into tears. " 'There's good in all of us, and I simply think I love people too much'—So why didn't you just fucking *stay?* —'so much that it makes me feel too fucking sad. The sad little sensitive unappreciative Pisces Jesus man.' Oh, shut up, bastard. 'Why don't you just enjoy it? I don't know.'

"Then he goes on to say personal things to me that are none

of your damn business, personal things to Frances that are none of your damn business[1] . . . 'I have it good, very good, and I'm grateful. But since the age of seven, I've become hateful toward all humans in general only because it seems so easy for people to get along and have empathy'—*empathy?*—'only because I love and feel sorry for people too much, I guess. Thank you all from the pit of my burning, nauseous stomach for your letters and concern during the past years. I'm too much of an erratic, moody person, and I don't have the passion anymore, so remember—' "

Courtney's voice sharpened. "And *don't* remember this, because this is a fucking lie. 'It's better to burn out than to fade away.' God, you asshole.

" 'Peace, love, empathy,

" 'Kurt Cobain.'

"And then there's some more personal things that are none of your damn business. And just remember, this is all bullshit. But I want you to know one thing. That eighties tough-love bullshit—it doesn't work. It's not real. It doesn't work. I should have let him, we all should have let him have his numbness. We should have let him have the thing that made him feel better, that made his stomach feel better, we should have let him have it instead of trying to strip away his skin. You go home and you tell your parents, 'Don't you ever try that tough-love bullshit on me, because it doesn't fucking work.' That's what I think."

She was sobbing by this time, but managed to finish. "I'm laying in our bed, and I'm really sorry, and I feel the same way you do. I'm really sorry, you guys. I don't know what I could have done. I wish I'd have been here. I wish I hadn't listened to other

---

[1] Courtney elaborated on this in a *Rolling Stone* interview in December 1994: "He wrote me a letter other than his suicide note. It's kind of long. I put it in a safe-deposit box. I might show it to Frances—maybe. It's very fucked-up writing. 'You know I love you, I love Frances, I'm so sorry. Please don't follow me.' It's long because he repeats himself. 'I'm sorry, I'm sorry, I'm sorry. I'll be there, I'll protect you. I don't know where I'm going. I just can't be here anymore.' "

people. But I did. Every night I've been sleeping with his mother, and I wake up in the morning and I think it's him because their bodies are sort of the same.

"I have to go now. Just tell him he's a fucker, okay? Just say, 'Fucker, you're a fucker.' And that you love him."

Her chest was sore, her face swollen from crying. Her stomach churned with guilt and nausea. She dragged herself to the memorial for Kurt's family and friends, attended mostly by record industry insiders. Courtney read from the Book of Job, the Book of Illuminations, and Kurt's note. Later that night she and Kat visited the Seattle Center, where a few ragged mourners still huddled over their candles. Courtney distributed some of Kurt's clothing to these faithful.

Live Through This was released the next day.

◇

Live Through This is a richly textured collage of an album, full of

strange juxtapositions: harsh and melodic, sarcastic and painfully

candid, pretty and ugly. Its lyrics are rife with images of dismem-

berment, pregnancy, birth, milk, sickness, nakedness. *Spin* called

it everything from "joyously gut-churning" to "the first great riot

grrrl sell-out manifesto."

Of course, all anyone heard in the weeks after its release were

the Kurt references, real and imagined. It was impossible to hear

181

Courtney sing "If you live through this with me I swear that I will die for you" without experiencing a frisson of terrible inevitability. She would later tell MTV's Kurt Loder, "I'm not psychic, but my lyrics are."

Strangest of all was a song that didn't make it onto the album, the original "Rock Star." When they decided to remove the track, it was too late to change the artwork. They substituted a song that they'd been calling "Olympia," but the title "Rock Star" made it onto the sleeve. The real lyrics to "Rock Star" went as follows:

How'd you like to be a rock star?
Lots of fun to be a rock star
I think you'd rather die
but I bet you'd like to try.
How'd you like to be in Nirvana?
Barrel of laughs to be in Nirvana
How'd you like to be in Nirvana?
I think you'd rather die.

Hole had planned to go on a U.S. tour in May. To no one's surprise, they canceled it. Instead, Courtney stayed in Seattle. She wrote some music with Kat—dreadful, raw, cathartic stuff. "She was the only person I could really play with except for Kurt," Courtney said later. "After all these years Kat and I still have our chemistry. It's fucking magic." At one point they let in a bunch of kids from the park across the street, which had become an unofficial shrine to Kurt. One boy had a guitar, and Courtney, Kat, and the kids went up to the greenhouse and sang all three Nirvana records straight through, as loud as they could.

She did a haunting photo shoot dressed in a vintage ballet costume. The pictures, by Mark Seliger, appeared in the May/June issue of *American Photo*. "We went to a beautiful mansion in Chicago," Courtney said in the accompanying text. "Mark is my favorite photographer, because he knows exactly how to make me feel.

This was pretty soon after the death of my husband. I became obsessed with angels and ballerinas, things of grace and beauty, otherworldly. I used all my ninth-grade ballet classes to do (bad) en pointe photos. I kept crying about every fifteen minutes, so I was a makeup nightmare. I wanted to be the swan in *Swan Lake* and flutter, crumple, and disappear. Mark got that on film."

Courtney made it through May by staying on the move. Spring in Seattle is achingly beautiful, bursting with life. The beauty sickened her. Before leaving home, she placed some of Kurt's ashes under a Buddha sculpture in the bedroom and buried some beneath a baby weeping willow tree in the front yard. Then she packed her wedding dress and the remainder of the ashes in a backpack shaped like a teddy bear, flew to New York City, and made a pilgrimage to the Namgyal Buddhist monastery in Ithaca.

At the airport security check, a guard opened the backpack. "What's this?" he asked upon seeing the quantity of gritty whitish powder.

"That's my husband," Courtney told him.

Courtney spent two weeks in the rugged hills of Ithaca, making herself infamous among the town's shopkeepers (Ithaca Guitar Works still displays one of her cigarette butts smudged with purple lipstick) and taking part each morning in the monks' ceremonies to consecrate the ashes. At last the backpack was opened and the ashes shaken out onto a table in a pale cloud that drifted around their heads. "We inhaled a little bit of Kurt that day," an attendant said. The ashes were placed upon the altar at the monastery.

When Courtney left Ithaca, two handfuls of Kurt's ashes stayed behind with the monks. After the consecration process was complete, the ashes would be mixed with clay and shaped into *tsatsas*, or Buddhist memorial sculptures.

Courtney flew to L.A. to attend the MTV Movie Awards with Michael Stipe, her first public appearance since Kurt's death. Other than that, she stayed holed up at home with Frances, who was beginning to understand—and protest—the fact that her father wasn't coming back. She had tantrums that ended in long, wrenching sobs. She screamed for him in the night. Once, while visiting a museum, she saw a tapestry of Jesus and called it "Daddy." Courtney tried to do the one thing no one had done for her when she was hurting as a child: she talked to Frances honestly in a way that Frances could understand. She said Daddy had to go away, and she didn't know why, but he was an angel now and he was watching them. Over and over she told Frances, "Daddy still loves you."

During her spell as a hermit, Courtney also spent a lot of time on the Internet. Jennifer Finch had sent her a used laptop computer, and Courtney went ego-surfing to see what everyone was saying about her, then began joining in the discussions on America Online. Her typing was terrible, which led readers to assume she was fucked up all the time; sometimes her disjointed posts read like surrealist poetry.

Many of her posts were scathing dismissals of the Olympia riot grrrls:

> Lois maffeo is 32, average age of bk [Bikini Kill] members is 25–29, funniest moment at a rg la hapter meeting; from a 36 yr old teacher at Riverside state college and i believe a cpa, "were taking the word back" she said, gee can we work on bitch, ho, cunt etc. note to bk drummer miss vail; "kim gordons old enuf to be my mother" yeah, if shed have had you when she was 11. sorry to burst yr tiny bubbles.
>
> [Kurt] was too afraid of getting reamed and ass-fucked by psychos like marylou[1] and tobyvale and cal-

---

[1] Mary Lou Lord, a singer who may or may not have dated Kurt, slept with Kurt, or given Kurt a single drunken blowjob in the back of a van, depending upon whom you believe. In 1995, Courtney chased Lord out of a backstage area and down a street, but did not catch her.

vin/candass the orig. diet grrl—people that would trade on his name to get major label deals, claim to co-author "teen spirit" a sophisticated pop song, when said claimants cannot tune, write, or show any spart of musical ingenuity.

To a detractor, she wrote,

thats the whole point dumbass,i wanna be there all alone center stage of Lolla, 43.000 people and be stoned, covered in blood beerpiss tomatoes your own sputum and urine,Dave,a mass stoning, Historical non? i wonder . . . would you be looking each other in the eyes or straight ahead,in a sort of Dionysian mass hypnosis?the way i saw the girl being passed around during 'Rape Me' in Ogden Utah from the side of the stage,they were all staring straightahead . . . as they ripped her shirt,bra, pants-grungey sort of shants ac- taully—panties—as they started mangling her breasts . . . hands on either side—her face was all screwed up in a scream—and the men were all glazed—AND STARING STRAIGHT AHEAD—my eyes fol- lowed a particularly violent boob mangling hand down to its owner—a baby faced grunge punque rocquer— at wich point i grabbed Novaselic and screamed and pointed—he jumped into the crowd and Kurt had the houselights turned on—i could only point out the cute boy for sure and the girl was bloody and hysterical— her breasts and stomach looked as though shed been clawed by jackels and Hungry Ghosts,from the coldest hell of the Bardo's.

Other posts attacked Hank Harrison, who had his own AOL presence and was using it to punish Courtney for refusing to let him meet Frances. Hank claimed he was going to write a tell-all book about Kurt and Courtney, a book that revealed what had *really* happened to Kurt.

Courtney wrote,

the man is nuts, and it goes far beyond a normal private fuedthere is no private relationship only the stark pathetic fact that he is using aol to pry his usual petty trade petty theft; just ak the grateful dead if my facts are straight, he claims to have managed thier charity events for an annum, pretty vague job description, but last time i checked he was still selling 60s dead boots in the back of relix gold mine and sometimes rolling stone and he had published 2 unauthorized books about this brief and disputed year, writing from the perspective of an insider, when in fact he barely dealt with the band, i know that i should pity him because he is old and youd think hed have calmed down, learned some humility, learned something positive to do with his brain, and he certainly is a witty man, but it just not true, hes crazy as a coot, he was in the 60 and he still is, and his ego is the same size, crazy and most people believe dangerous . . . im home, surrounded by a much needed 24 hour security, thats so sick, we NEED this, a new cyclone electronic fence w sensors, a rottweiler a german shepard and a baby chowdog for the bean. id like to add that fatdaddy aka biodad tried to enter the house and grounds, he told eric my guitarist that i said he could come over, as well as "sanctioning" his lovely Geraldo Appearance, HOW SCARY IS THAT GENERAL PUBLIC'AOL READERS?

He said he'd saved 2000 lives in the last two months, yeah rights as said if only, the ones writing me were suicidal . . . im locked in a moat with the ugliest fence money can buy, and its no longer charming guileless KIDS NOW IT IS THE LEGITIMATELY intensely insane people . . the ones wriimg THOSE letters, the ones in blood, the satan ones,

a note to all you biographers out there;

YOU ARE ALL WRITING ME THE SAME LETTER

AND AT THIS POINT YOU ARE ALL MALE. i wish i could show you all the form letter you are sending, the vaguelt threatening tone, the 'This book WILL be written platitude and the im the guy to do it blanket statement, as if you think somewhere between striking the right chord and provoking me with the wrong one you can gleefully rush into the alleged publishers office with "IVE GOT HER" written all over tr face, gee as a buch of writers with no actual publishing deals yet you should get some tips from biodad, there is nothing you can do to me to ellicit a response, positive (as in azzerad) or better negative—like the Clarke*collins very public debacle wich explains the smarmy provacaive statements . . . im not as stupid as the dozen of you think, ive been through this, if i smack you upside yr head, well then im just giving you all the fiery tabloid fodder youll need to set up yr marketing campaigns, and if i open my home and heart to you, ill get screwed, no duh, yes boys this book WILL GET WRITTEN COURTNEY

And so will 300yhty ones and i chris and dave dont care, weve gone thru this so much we dont care I DONT

Caaaaaaaaaaaaaaaaaaaaaaaa

RRRRRRRREEEEEEEEEOK?

theres nothing left of me fffffffffffffffff
vmmmmmmm

mmmmmmmmmmmmmmmmmmmmmmmmmm
mmmmmmmmmmmmmmmmmmmmmmmmmmmm
mmmmmmmmmmmmmmmmmmmmmmmmmmmm
mmmmmmmmmmmmmmmmmmmmmmmmmmmm
mmmmmmmmmmmmmmmmmmmmmmmmmmmm
mmmmmmmmmmmmmmmmmmmmmmmmmmmm
mmmmmmmmmmmmmmmmmmmmmmmmmmmm
mmmmmmmmmmmmmmmmmmmmmmmmmmmm
mmmmmmmmmmmmmmmmmmmmmmmmmmmm
mmmmmmmmmmmmmmmmmmmmmmmmmmmm
mmmmmmmmmmmmmmmmmmmmmmmmmmmm
mmmmmmmmmmmmmmmmmmmmmmmmmmmm
mmmmmmmmmmmmmmmmmmmmmmmmmmmm
mmmmmmmmmmmmmmmmmmmmmmmmmmmm
mmmmmmmmmmmmmmmmmmmmmmmmmmmm
mmmmmmmmmmmmmmmmmmmmmmmmmmmm
mmmmmmmmmmmmmmmmmmmmmmmmmmmm
mmmmmmmmmmmmmmmmmmmmmmmmmmmm
mmmmmmmmmmmmmmmmmmmmmmmmmmmm
mmmmmmmmmmmmmmmmmmmmmmmmmmmm
mmmmmmmmmmmmmmmmmmmmmmmmmmmm
mmmmmmmmmmmmmmmmmmmmmmmmmmmm
mmmmmmmmmmmmmmmmmmmm

She discovered another hostile presence on the Internet: Tom
Grant, a private investigator she had briefly hired to look for Kurt
during his last days. Grant had developed a theory that Kurt had
been murdered by agents of Courtney. He offered two implausible motives: Kurt had wanted to divorce Courtney, and Kurt's
death would boost Courtney's career. When the Seattle police
wouldn't listen to him, Grant took his case to talk radio, then the
British tabloids, then cyberspace. There he hooked up with Hank

Harrison, who embraced Grant's theory so warmly that the two of them managed to get it written up in the venerable stoner rag *High Times.*

The two later feuded, but nothing stopped Grant; the Cobain case has become his raison d'être. When last heard from, he was running an anti-Courtney web page and peddling a book.

On June 13, Courtney called a meeting of her band. They established that nobody wanted to quit, but agreed to take a two-month break and go on tour in the fall. Kristen Pfaff wanted to take an extended vacation in Minneapolis, visit old friends, and play some gigs with her old band, Janitor Joe. "I pretty much laid it out," Pfaff had told a reporter a month earlier. "I said [to my band], 'Look, if you want me to be happy and sane, I just need to get back home.' "

On the night of June 15, 1994, she had a small going-away party at her Capitol Hill apartment. When everyone had left, she ran herself a bath, injected herself with heroin, and slipped into the tub.

Eric found her slumped in the cold water the next morning, head and arms draped over the side of the tub, black hair hanging down in a ragged curtain. She had died of an overdose. Kristen was twenty-seven, the same age Kurt had been.

Kristen's funeral was a textbook example of two cultures failing to communicate. Her father, Norm Pfaff, felt that her Seattle friends were uncommunicative and uncaring. He mistook what was probably a massive pall of guilt for a glaze of indifference.

"Her friends from Minneapolis had conveyed their sincere condolences to me, and I had met some of them previous to her death," he told music columnist Jim Walsh of the *St. Paul Pioneer Press.* "And I was just comparing that to the response I was seeing from the people in Seattle. To be fair, there wasn't much contact. I'm talking about two or three people. So the comment might not have been totally fair. But just as an example, Eric was at the postfuneral gathering and didn't even say a word to me. And then again, I'm not saying that Eric didn't care about Kristen, but to me there was a noticeable difference in the response."

He didn't add that the Minneapolis friends were able to take the moral high ground, while the Seattleites were miserably afraid that the Minneapolis friends were right: their city had killed Kristen.

"Don't you get embarrassed that Seattle is famous for grunge, cappuccino, and heroin?" Courtney had asked the city cops after Kurt's death. But she wasn't at Kristen's funeral: the family had asked that the other members of Hole not attend, and only Eric had defied the ban. And as much as she'd loved Kristen, Courtney felt that she had very little sorrow left for anybody; she was drained, numb.

Together, she, Eric, and Patty decided not to break up the band. They started auditioning bass players. When Billy Corgan recommended Melissa Auf Der Maur, a twenty-two-year-old from Montreal, Courtney was skeptical. "Billy was going on about this hot babe who could really play, and I was like, 'Yeah, right, you're giving her the girl leeway,' because Billy is sort of a pig," she said later. "But I thought I would try her out, and I pursued her a little bit, and what I thought was hot was that she said no."

"That's a thing to like," Melissa responded. "That's attractive. Yeah, I was just, like, in my space, in my life, with my band [Tinker]. I had been at the New Music Seminar handing out my demo tapes and putting my seven-inch together. I was like, 'No way, I've got my life—what, you think I wanna leave my life?' "

But Courtney's charisma was back big-time; she believed that going on tour, *working*, was the only thing that would save her. To do that, she needed Melissa. And, in the end, she got Melissa, who remained unfazed by it all: two weeks after her audition, facing an audience of eighty thousand at the 1994 Reading Festival, Melissa commented, "I felt nothing. I was like, 'This is just a reflection of what I'm about to do with my life.' "

Courtney has described the August 26 show at Reading as "chaotic." She wore a gold dress and looked unsteady on her feet. "Oh yeah, I'm so goddamn brave," she snarled at the crowd. "Let's just pretend it didn't happen. Oh yeah. This is like a hobby for me." The crowd returned her hostility, and the press skewered her.

The next day, she commented, "The vibe to me was like goddess worship on the verge of stoning me to death. It was really freaky and I ignored it. I don't know what they wanted, but I ignored it. In fact, I know what they wanted, and I wasn't gonna give them that. It was strange. Usually every fucking time I play, someone says, 'Show us your tits.' I was so ready for them. I had on my Wonderbra. We just went and played a tight set . . . What did they want? A fucking cover of 'Teen Spirit'? I don't understand it. Were people curious as a freak thing? I think they wanted me to cry, and I won't."

And she wouldn't. Courtney was farther down than she had ever been, but she was starting to crawl back from the depths.

Then she met the perfect person to take her straight down again.

◇

CHAPTER TWENTY - ONE

Nine Inch Nails' 1989 album *Pretty Hate Machine* was the same

kind of unanticipated runaway success that *Nevermind* would be

two years later. The music, an agonized fusion of industrial, goth,

and synth-pop, was written entirely by Trent Reznor. He also

sang and played most of the instruments. In his lyrics, Reznor

dissected a lost love, decried the ugliness of the human condition,

and castigated himself for being alive. Even Kurt, who normally

hated anything popular, had listened to *Pretty Hate Machine* and said things like, "This song could be so great if there wasn't any synthesizer on it."

Trent Reznor himself was a strange beauty, angular and pale, with sunken eyes as intense as Kurt's but nowhere near as innocent. He wore his hair in long, jet-black masses that framed his thin face, exaggerating his pallor. He recorded his second full-length album, *The Downward Spiral,* in the L.A. house where the Manson family slaughtered five people (including *Valley of the Dolls* starlet Sharon Tate) and wrote on the walls in their blood.

In September, NIN asked Hole to open several shows on their tour for *The Downward Spiral.* Hole agreed to the tour. At the first show, in Cleveland, Courtney received a death threat. "The chief of police came down and told me that he didn't want me to play," she said. "I'm like, 'It's from a girl, it's bullshit.' Besides, if someone were to shoot me onstage, what a nice footnote to rock'n'roll history."

Trent later claimed that Courtney was "completely intoxicated, a fucking mess" at that first show, and she admits it. According to other witnesses on the tour, that didn't stop him from moving in on her. He invited her to his room one night, saying he had something for her (in *Details,* later, he would claim it was some herb tea for her throat).

"I could kick Trent's ass through honesty," Courtney commented after the tour. "Or at least come out even. I'm pathologically competitive with men. Nine Inch Nails had the lights and the technology; I was so scared we'd eat shit, but it worked out very smoothly. Too smoothly, if you ask me. I'm glad it was only a short tour. I started raveling, internally.

"It was fun to play with some of the imagery, to pander to that audience. I got to wear black onstage, which I have never done in my life. And then I worked my thing to death. I put my hair in ringlets every fucking night. I did my Baby-Jane-fuck-you sick thing every fucking night. In Minneapolis, I wore a dress that was so restricting and shoes that were five inches high, I could barely stage-dive. Then I got like the best write-ups—for being feminine, I guess. I couldn't move well and I was restrained, which equals great review. That's pretty horrid."

She didn't elaborate on "too smoothly" or "raveling, internally," but many of the people around her believed it had to do with Trent.

Hole continued their tour. During the fall 1994 shows, Courtney cursed the crowd, baptized them by spitting water, and flung baby dolls at them. If they were good, she sometimes brought Frances onstage for them to see. She improvised new lyrics to old songs, changing a line from "Miss World" to "I am the girl you know / The one who should have died," or a line in "I Think That I Would Die" to "I want him / He's all gone." She dived from the stage almost every night, borne on the groping hands of the crowd, her eyes wide and impassive, her limbs stiff as her clothes were shredded and her body battered. Watching Courtney stage-dive now was like watching a woman do a painful penance.

In September, Courtney commented to MTV's Kurt Loder about having gone back to work so soon after Kurt's death. "I think that it's expected that I should go close the drapes and, you know, shoot drugs or something for, you know, five years. But I don't want to do that. You know, I have a baby, I have to make a living . . . it's the one time I feel really good."

She also spoke of her late husband's continued presence in her life. "I know that wherever he is, a lot's dissipated, but there's a major guilt left behind. And he's got to have his dignity restored, and his true self. And he could be a real grumpy bastard, but that was part of his power. You know, without saying a word he could make the whole room feel like shit . . . And he also had an intense narcissism, like, 'You're coming to me.' But he didn't have one *atom* of rock-star ego, and he needed it."

She had plenty of rock-star ego in her life now. As if whatever relationship she had with Trent wasn't enough, she, or someone posting under her name, had gotten into more trouble on-line. On September 4, the following message was posted under her name:

> uhhh . . grohl has JOINED PEARL JAM. this will undoubetly be pubished but i dont fucking care,fyi, Kurt was not on speaking terms w/ Dve Iscariot anyway 4 over a year, fuck him, yeah fuck you dave, ill be yr fuckin Yoko nightmare you fucking traitor . . . Thanks for not even calling after Rome, thanks for being a fuck you hve now made lifes rich shit list; the company of albini,mike D(cum Silva),Hershberg and the loverly Tina Brown—get those Jeremy royalties dave, Fuck you, why didnt you just join the fucking cult . . . God you are LOW and KC would juest shrug ,im sure he wouldnt be surprised anyeway . . . . i like doing this on the Void, better than ever speaking to you again . . . . . im going w/Stipe to the aewards, lets maake those rumours finally cum true,uck you dave,shoot some hoop w/ jeffy ok? fucker.

Two days later, another message appeared:

> hi carol [the woman who forwarded her posts] this is Courtney . . . I did not hear of David Grohl Joining Pearl Jam and even if he didits really his life and his business, Ive noticed postings lately that our not mine—carried over by you—i ama ware that I gave you full pemission to do this—but how could someone use my email, i mean my passwod is pretty obvious— it wouldnt take a ROCKET SCIENTIST to figure it out . . . in the laast 24 hours 2 people i respect—one whom i really love and value have accused me of being a liar—you know that feeling—when you didnt do

something . Well i didnt post to you about Dave Grohl Joiining Pearl Jam and i would not be classless ee-nough to do this anyway—to be honest i would not really care—its his life. anyway the media will be all over this yesterday and i dont need it and neither does Dave, I love Dave. I love Krist. Now they are madat me they think I did this thing—and they think im lying, im not and id like you to help me get to the bottom of it because theres nothing more frustrating and at this point PAINFUL than having people think you did stuff you didnt do, post this near the faux Courtney posting—or remove it if you can or help me figure out who did this—alright Carol thanks,Im re-ally sorry this happened ,the Courtney Crazy signature writing really pissses me off too, about 8–9 days ago you sent me a postng i had allegedly sent you.,that I had not writtten, i didnt respond as it was innocous—i thought it was more making fun of my crazy Joycean -smack addled writing "style"—also i got a fanzine called "Mad Love" that had fraudulent postings—not many, but a few—pls from now on confirm with me before going over to the net if its something as cazed and destructive as that was—by the way Dave was very supportive after Rome, I dont need people i love calling me a liar as this will obligate me to rather despise them—and i dont want any of this shit crazy anger—thanks Carol . . . . Courtney

In the end, it was impossible to sort out which posts were really Courtney and which weren't—she did have several imper-sonators. But it is generally believed that she really did write the (untrue) post about Dave Grohl joining Pearl Jam, then thought better of it.

Meanwhile, she and Trent rendezvoused first in New Orleans,

then in L.A. In the sprawling city of angels, their relationship died a sudden, ugly death.

Together at the Sunset Marquis Hotel (or as Courtney would later call it, the "Marquis de Sunset"), they got into a fight. According to a person on Hole's staff, the fight was about "something very bad Trent had done, that Courtney would never talk about." Trent allegedly left the room for several hours, then came back just before dawn and accused Courtney of going through his things, of trashing the room, of everything but boiling his pet rabbit.

They had a loud argument, and Courtney turned to leave. What she saw when she opened the door sucked out all her fire, destroyed her more thoroughly than anything since the sight of Kurt's blood on the greenhouse floor.

Trent had stationed two bodyguards outside the room—two "goons," as Courtney's AOL posts later referred to them. Her heart sank as she realized that *this* was what Trent thought of her. He had treated her as a peer, a colleague, a friend. But in the end, he'd called the goons to get rid of her, just as she'd heard he did to groupies he was tired of.

She left the hotel, went to another, checked in under a pseudonym, and took a sleeping pill. When she woke up, the empty side of the bed was there to greet her like an old friend.

Rumors of their affair had already surfaced in the media. Now *People* got hold of the Sunset Marquis story, only in their version Courtney had done four thousand dollars' worth of damage to the hotel and Trent had beaten her up, leaving bruises. Soon Courtney was relating her own version of events on her AOL folder: "lousylaylousylaylouseylaye what i have paid in blood and dishonour for that lousy lay." She described the scene backstage at a typical NIN show, claiming that groupies were passed around, degraded, roughed up, and even raped, often without ever getting close to "Ratboy" himself. She made fun of his silver Porsche.

When people heckled her about Trent onstage, she said things like, "Nine Inch Nails? More like Three Inch Nails."

(Another well-known pop diva is rumored to have suffered even worse treatment at Trent's hands. According to one source, "They met in L.A., she dropped her boyfriend for him, she had the keys to his house in New Orleans. She went over there one day and all the locks were changed. She called from her car phone, and the number was changed. Then she was standing there on the sidewalk wondering what the hell was going on, and Trent had two bodyguards come out and throw her into her car. I believe he gets off on humiliating powerful women.")

When word of Courtney's on-line activity leaked out, Trent responded in the press by claiming that the affair had never taken place at all. Courtney had gotten mad because "I wouldn't be her boyfriend," he said, and, "It just wasn't gonna happen—the romance of the century."

To Courtney, this was as much of a slap as the goons at the Sunset Marquis had been. What had happened between them was ugly enough—but to *deny* it? Nothing could be colder. She redoubled her Internet harangues, and her AOL folder became a thing of morbid fascination, like an unfolding postmortem.

And, like any protracted carrion-gnawing, it drew flies. In November, a presence called Sasha (also known as S23, Taran, and several other aliases) appeared on AOL and began savaging Courtney and anyone who dared speak a kind word about her. Sasha was articulate, vicious, and madly in love/hate with Trent Reznor. She goaded Courtney to reveal more details of NIN's backstage squalor, saying Courtney had "promised" to do so. When Courtney declined, Sasha became a very vocal proponent of Tom Grant's conspiracy theory.

For a while Courtney thought Sasha was really "Crazy Amy," an ex-girlfriend of Trent's who had tracked her down after the breakup, pretended to make friends with her, and taken sadistic pleasure in revealing all sorts of lies Trent had told Courtney during the course of their relationship. Rumors circulated on-line that Sasha was actually Kat Bjelland, Mary Lou Lord, or even Jennifer Finch.

(The following year, Sasha posted a death threat against another AOL member. Some people say she also sent one to Courtney via private e-mail. The Hole folder was closed, Sasha was kicked off AOL, and Courtney hired an attorney to find her. According to the attorney, who seems to have acted in the capacity of a private investigator, Sasha was a sad character. A fat goth in her mid-thirties, she lived with her parents in a dismal suburb of San Francisco. She bragged on-line about trips she was going to take to Prague, Rome, and Japan, but an arthritic condition in her legs and feet prevented her from walking long distances. She appeared to live completely through her Internet persona. Sasha, or someone using her name, is still active on the Net; her vitriolic posts may be found on the Usenet group alt.fan.courtney-love.)

That fall, Nine Inch Nails canceled an appearance at Madison Square Garden. The story from the NIN camp was that the guitarist had injured his hand. Unofficially, it was said that Trent had canceled the show because he heard that Courtney was going to be there. She *had* planned to attend—along with Evan Dando, Eric, and his new girlfriend, actress Drew Barrymore. Word was that Trent had expected her to come backstage and cause a scene. Each fresh piece of news seemed more carefully designed to stab her through the heart, but she found that she was getting used to it, just a little. She wondered if there was anything she *couldn't* get used to.

Late in 1994, she started putting together the soundtrack for the movie *Tank Girl,* which had been (abysmally) adapted from a British comic about a punk superheroine of the future and her kangaroo boyfriend. The soundtrack would include songs by

Björk, Veruca Salt, and Hole, who contributed "Drown Soda," recorded live at the BBC.

Just before Christmas, while Nine Inch Nails were still on tour, Trent's beloved pet dog fell over a fifty-foot railing at a show and died. Courtney was said to have cried all day when she heard the news, but couldn't bring herself tell anyone what had upset her so badly.

She spent Christmas at home with Frances, who was recovering from chicken pox.

Early in 1995, Hole toured Australia, where a statement Courtney had often made about herself was proved yet again:

"I just hold up my finger and shit sticks to it."

CHAPTER TWENTY-TWO

◇

Sitting in an Australian police station, Courtney penned the following letter to Qantas Airways:

I have just got off flight 627 from Brisbane to Melbourne, where I flew first class in seat 1F. I am at present being detained by Victoria police over a petty and pathetic incident instigated by a stewardess whose name was Veronica Mahony. I found her behavior unusual from the start. A. She pulled out everyone in first class's dinner trays without asking them at all. B. When I refused to have dinner, she became slightly hostile for no apparent reason.

I had just spent 2½ hours in the sickroom at Brisbane Airport. I have lumbar strain, sciatica and am also quite ill at the moment with a high temperature and hot chills. I put my feet up on the bulkhead wall as well as a pillow under my back. As I am a regular first-class flier I usually sit in 1G aisle seat—bulkhead. And this is normal behavior. She confronted me about this and said I was A. offending other passengers (feet on wall—offending passengers?) and B. caused a security problem because the wall was in front of some secure/safety "device" (it is in fact in front of catering).

I am a celebrity and at this point she noticed a magazine (*Rolling Stone*) on the floor which I was on the cover of. This has happened to me many, many times—somewhere between just being a celebrity and the nature of my celebrity—a rock singer. However, I have not, in 28 years of flying, EVER encountered a problem in my in-flight activities nor a stewardess so shrill, nasty, and flat-out mean. Sometimes people like to have altercations/confrontations with celebrities. It gives them a sense of their own worth—I'm not a mind reader but from the moment she saw that magazine her attitude became increasingly nasty. The passenger next to me even commented on this.

She told me to get my feet down. I said "why?" She said the 2 things I told you. I said, "I've never heard of that"—she repeated herself, "Get your feet down"—from the start, no "please," no "politeness," no pleasant way of informing me this was perhaps wrong. Just nasty and rude. I said, "NO, my back hurts and I've never heard of this rule." She said (and I repeat in an extremely <u>rude</u> tone of voice) "Get them down or I'll have you arrested at the airport." I was furious and I said, "Go the fuck ahead" . . .

The next hour or so of the flight was fine. No more altercations. I removed my feet eventually as my back stopped hurting so much. When we got to Melbourne it looked as though the cavalry was there! I saw at least 6, maybe more, officials—security and police. I have so far been detained for over an hour and strip-searched. (Fortunately the police conducting this are about 2000 times more polite than the stewardess.)

I didn't break the law, become inebriated, become belligerent or rude except in an offhanded way to this exceptionally nasty stewardess. I am willing to BET that this will be on the Associated Press wire within an hour. And I am also willing to bet that it won't come from these police but from the stewardess herself.

I have heard of drunk people smoking cigarettes and pot on planes, urinating outside of cubicles. Bad things. <u>I PUT MY FEET UP ON THE BULK-HEAD WALL!!</u> and have as a consequence been humiliated beyond almost any experience. Your airline has always been a good one. I fly my employees and band on it.

You have turned this into a "criminal matter" and in your report your stewardess outright <u>lied,</u> i.e. that I raised my hand as if to STRIKE HER . . . or that I locked myself in a bathroom and wouldn't come out. These are <u>all</u> outright lies . . . I have been offended beyond belief.

It turned out that she *had* broken the law: apparently it was illegal to say "fuck" on an Australian airplane. She was released after posting bail.

When the tour was over, Courtney flew to Japan to visit a Buddhist monastery in Nagoya. The night before her pilgrimage, she started having cold sweats. The next day at the monastery, a priest told her to rid herself of all hatred. She resolved to try.

Back in the States, Courtney called Trent. He touches upon their conversation in the April 1995 issue of *Details:* "She seemed somewhat genuinely to want to make up. And I don't want a war between us. I said, 'If you want it to be stopped, stop it.' . . . There's a nice side to her, and that's what I saw today. She's certainly a fucking character."

But he had already said several nasty things about Courtney to the *Details* writer, as well as repeating his denial of their sexual relationship. All of this was included in the article, and Courtney abandoned her mission of peace. In upcoming months, Trent was referred to in the Hole camp as "the vermin."

In the spring of 1995, Courtney bought a $400,000 house for Wendy O'Connor, Kurt's mother. She got a couple of small movie roles: a waitress in *Feeling Minnesota* with Keanu Reeves; an art groupie called Big Pink in *Basquiat,* the eponymous biopic of Andy Warhol prodigy Jean-Michel Basquiat. She saw *Live Through This* fail to get nominated for a Grammy award, despite unanimous critical acclaim and sales edging up toward a million. The sting was assuaged by an invitation to fill a major slot on the 1995 Lollapalooza tour, headlined by Sonic Youth.

She also found a new best friend: Amanda DeCadenet, a hard-partying British girl whose marriage to Duran Duran's John Taylor was eclipsed by her own glitzy image. "Amanda is a star-fucker," says an old friend of Courtney's, "and Courtney was just another star. It didn't matter that she was a girl, it didn't matter that they never had sex. Amanda hung on to her like a starfucker." Courtney would later drop Amanda like a hot rock, characterizing her as "pathological."

In March, still in their honeymoon phase, they attended the Academy Award ceremonies in tiaras and long dresses of white silk charmeuse, kissed for the cameras, and generally had fun disgracing themselves. At one of the after-parties, they visited Quentin Tarantino's table, and Courtney found herself sitting next to Lynn Hirschberg.

"I'm picking up the Oscar," she told Chicago radio station WKQF later, "and they're really heavy, because they're lead with gold over it. You could totally brain somebody. I'm like, 'Who do I hate in this room?' All of a sudden this little voice peeps up . . . 'You don't like me.' . . . And she bolted and she hid under Madonna and Ellen Barkin and Jodie Foster's table, and they were kicking her under the table. Jodie Foster was smoking cigars and putting them out on her and screaming, 'Face the music, bitch!' . . . Had I punched her, they'd just say, 'There goes Courtney again.' But I kept my poise."

As if this incident—and the fact that Hirschberg had cancer —was not enough to satisfy Courtney's sense of karma, *Vanity Fair* contacted her about doing a cover story. The interview would be conducted not by a freelancer, but by contributing editor Kevin Sessums, who adored her.

The June 1995 cover of *Vanity Fair* could not have been a more literal apology for the 1992 article. Exquisitely made up and dreamy-faced, in a tight peach-colored dress and white-feathered angel wings, Courtney was shown stepping out of an ornate golden picture frame. The story was accompanied by several seminude portraits of her, and an exquisite one of Frances Bean staring into the camera, her father's soul clearly reflected in her huge, knowing eyes.

"The American public really does have a death wish for me," Courtney told Sessums. "They want me to die. I'm not going to die."

Hole did a brief tour of Europe that spring. In Amsterdam, the press reported that Courtney had shimmied up a balcony pole to chase out a female heckler at the Paradiso Club. A Dutch Internet surfer who claimed to have been in the audience gave another version of events. This person reported that the girl kept yelling, "You killed Kurt!" and when others began to follow suit, Courtney put down her guitar.

"Okay," she is reported to have said. "Good night. That's it. You girls shit on me, you don't get a fucking show . . . Are you mad because you think I fucked Trent? Are you mad because you think I fucked Evan? Are you mad because I married Kurt? Well, tough shit, you fat ugly goth. Go fuck yourself. Kurt hated this fucking town. I hate this town. Go fuck yourself! Go see Nine Inch Nails next time."

"You paid fucking money for this show, you fucking bitch!" Melissa Auf Der Maur reportedly chimed in.

Back in the States, Courtney very nearly fulfilled her American public's supposed death wish. She was taking a lot of pills that spring and summer: Percodans, Valiums, and many, many Rohypnols. On a June 11 flight from New York to Seattle, suddenly depressed, she swallowed three at once. Her assistant had to help her off the plane and load her into a taxi. By the time they got home, Courtney was unconscious, unresponsive, and hardly seemed to be breathing. The assistant called paramedics, who rushed her to Harborview Medical Center. Her stomach was pumped, her vital signs monitored for twelve hours.

By the time she was released at two o'clock the next afternoon, she couldn't get the *Valley of the Dolls* theme song out of her head. It had only been about half accidental.

◇

CHAPTER TWENTY - THREE

There were rumors that Hole would pull out of Lollapalooza, but

there Courtney was on opening day, July 3, "bleary-eyed" and

"sallow-faced" according to *Rolling Stone.*

Lollapalooza began in 1991 as a traveling festival of music,

arts, and various subcultures. It was founded by Perry Farrell,

then vocalist for Jane's Addiction. The 1995 lineup was the most

esoteric so far, featuring Pavement, Beck, Cypress Hill, the Jesus

Lizard, Sinéad O'Connor (who dropped out early due to

pregnancy), and Bikini Kill as well as Hole. Even the headlining act, Sonic Youth, was more a revered cult band than a rock legend.

On the very first day of the six-week tour, Courtney got in trouble. In her tour diary for *Spin,* she wrote,

> [Kathleen Hanna of Bikini Kill] was my husband's worst enemy in the world, someone who would stop at nothing to aggravate us . . . It's after our set—-before Sonic Youth's—and I'm onstage talking to Beck when Eric comes up and says, "Kathleen's behind you. You should give her some candy and freak her out." And there she was, sort of smirking at me. I dropped my sweater on the floor, and she sort of whispered under her breath, "Where's the baby? In the closet with an IV?" I just snapped. My hand was filled with Skittles, and a couple of Tootsie Rolls. I just threw them up in the air and went, "BAAAAAAAAAAAAAAA!" And then she shoved me and then I clocked her. This all happened within five seconds. These big bodyguards grab us, and we're both being lifted up, and she's screaming and screeching all sorts of things at me, and I was laughing at her, like, "Go feed the fucking homeless or something." I think I had a bag of tostadas as well, mixed in with the candy, so it was raining candy and tostadas everywhere. K.H. said that I attacked her and that I was on drugs and psychotic; you know, all the things that the hicks in Peoria would eat up. Then she went into Sonic Youth's room and tattled and told them this totally exaggerated, insane story about how I had attacked her out of the blue and sucker-punched her, when in fact I had nine or ten witnesses to the contrary . . .
>
> K.H. suffered no damage. I barely got to hit her.

Everybody in my band was really disgusted with her, as were those that had witnessed it, because a couple of people had heard what she'd said. She insulted my daughter in a very, very wicked and evil way. I actually had intended to give her the candy and walk away.

Kathleen Hanna pressed assault charges, and Courtney would end up with a one-year jail sentence, suspended on the condition that she take "anger-management classes" and refrain from punching anyone for two years.[1]

But Courtney got her aggression out early. For most of the tour she was subdued, sleeping a lot, watching movies in the back of her bus, medicating herself so heavily after the shows that cigarette-burn holes began to show up in her clothes, her bedding, and even on her skin, like when she'd been a junkie. She couldn't sleep without her pills, and when she'd been awake for too long, she started thinking about Kurt.

On the last day of July, someone threw a shotgun shell onstage halfway through Hole's set. The shell landed at Courtney's feet. When Courtney bent over and picked it up, the band stopped playing.

"Is this what you want?" Courtney asked, gazing out into the audience. "Okay. Good night. Thanks." Hole left the stage. Friends who visited Courtney on tour reported that she seemed lonely and depressed.

Courtney concluded her tour diary,

> Lolla helped wake me from my numbness. I'd been a zombie for 18 months. For so long in my marriage, and afterward, I'd been in isolation, oblivious to everything but my darkest hedonism and darkest hours. If

---

[1] Her good-behavior period ends September 27, 1997.

I'm ever going to write this new record, I have to feel
my heart again. I've gone back into therapy (Sinéad
convinced me), and I'm also on a diet from hell with
the help of a personal trainer for this film I'm up for.
This is all bringing me back to order at last—it's not
the exercise, it's the discipline. I'm finally returning
from the land of agoraphobia, trying to purge myself
of my vitriol for everyone that had ever hurt or exploited Kurt. I wonder if clocking somebody counts as
purging? Yeah, definitely, it counts.

"This film I'm up for" was her first shot at a major role in a
major motion picture. Director Milos Forman had seen an early
cut of *Feeling Minnesota*, and was so impressed that he asked
Courtney to test for his next picture. *The People vs. Larry Flynt*,
to be produced by Oliver Stone, was the story of the *Hustler*
publisher's rise to infamy, his court battle against censorship, and
the subsequent attempt on his life that left him in a wheelchair.
Along with actresses Patricia Arquette, Mira Sorvino, Rachel
Griffiths, and Georgina Cates, Courtney was up for the role of
Larry's wife, Althea Leasure Flynt. Seven years old when she saw
her father shoot her mother and her grandparents before turning
the gun on himself, barely legal when she met Larry, Althea
would have to age sixteen years in the course of the film.

Forman asked Courtney to come and meet him at the Sunset
Marquis in L.A. She hadn't been back there since Trent, since
the fight. She gathered up all her strength, all her charm, and set
out to regain lost territory.

According to *Premiere*, Milos Forman knew he wanted Courtney for the part before she had finished crossing the room. "She
is this wonderful combination," he said, "generous, fragile, loving,
determined, and tough."

When Forman showed the Althea screen tests to his longtime
friend, playwright and Czech Republic president Václav Havel,

Havel told him Courtney was the only choice. Oliver Stone was just as complimentary: "It was clear that she had primal energy. You needed somebody with balls to the sky [to play Althea]. She's got balls, this woman."

Larry Flynt himself wasn't so sure: he favored Ashley Judd for the role of his late wife. And the film's insurers were leery of covering an inexperienced actress with such a well-known drug history.

"For two months I was Althea, and I wasn't Althea, and I was, and I wasn't," Courtney told *Premiere*. "It was not even because of me so much as the baggage. I think they really thought I was gonna make beer pyramids in my trailer. Bring in the local crackheads and party down."

In the end, Courtney, Stone, Forman, and Woody Harrelson contributed $100,000 apiece for a separate "high-risk" insurance policy. Courtney would have to pass a urine test once a week for the duration of filming. She would be able to take medications prescribed to her—Valium, occasionally Percodan, and the odd antidepressant—but nothing else.

"I said, 'Oh, fuck it,' " she commented later, again to *Premiere*. "It's, like, my scarlet letter. My little cross to bear. I'm accountable for this on some level and I can't pretend to be oblivious . . . [But] I've ruined things for other people now. They're all gonna have to be taking tests."

That fall, Caroline Records released *Ask for It,* a Hole EP of live songs and John Peel sessions from BBC Radio. This EP was a contractual leftover from the deal they'd had with Caroline before they signed to Geffen. The stark cover art, selected by Courtney as always, depicted a pair of bloodless slit wrists splayed upon a bathroom floor. *Ask for It* included covers of songs by the Velvet Underground, the Wipers, the Germs, and even Calvin Johnson's band, Beat Happening, as sort of a half-friendly fuck-you.

Courtney filmed an interview with Barbara Walters that

would air later in the year. Dressed carefully in a pink Thierry Mugler suit, she broke down in tears several times as Walters fired questions at her. Was she on drugs? Right now? While pregnant? Did she use drugs in front of Frances? Did she blame herself for Kurt's suicide?

"That was *opera*," Courtney would later tell *Vogue*. "That woman is a Flaming Temptress. It was more than opera—it was Grand Guignol. It was gore theater and I was the leading lady and that is all. I did Lady Macbeth, all right? In front of twenty million people, there you go. You have to move on from there."

In October, Hole played "Violet" on the MTV Video Music Awards. At the post-Awards show, while Madonna was being interviewed by Kurt Loder, Courtney butted in and a very peculiar exchange took place on camera.

> Kurt Loder [to Madonna]: You have an album of ballads coming out, right?
> [We hear Courtney yelling, "Madonna!" in the background.]
> Madonna: Yeah, *Something to Remember*, something smoochie.
> KL: Something smoochie?
> M: Something to you-know-what to.
> KL: Does this reflect a new smoochiness in your life or . . .
> M: You may say it's um . . . a reflection of that . . . but it's also . . .
> [A powder compact whizzes past Madonna's head.]
> KL: Hi, Courtney! That's Courtney, everybody's favorite. Come on up.
> M: Should we let her come up? No, don't, please. Don't.

KL: Yeah, come on up. Courtney's coming up.

[Courtney is shown at the foot of the stage,
    grinning and still throwing makeup at
    Madonna.]

M: Courtney Love is in dire need of attention
    right now. She's throwing her compacts
    at me.

KL: I'll just stand here . . .

[Courtney takes the stage.]

Courtney Love [to Madonna]: Hi, how are you?

M: Good.

CL [shaking hands]: Whatcha doing?

M: I'm talking up here.

CL: Oh, am I, am I interrupting?

KL: No, no, we have some questions for you. Is this
    your first encounter?

M: No, no, we've met.

CL: We've had a few encounters.

KL [to Madonna]: Did you see Hole's performance?

M: I didn't see it.

CL: She didn't watch it.

KL: It's not like she didn't watch it, she probably
    just missed it.

M: I saw the rehearsal, though.

CL: We have our Maverick, you know . . . [a
    mysterious but clearly catty reference to
    Madonna's record label, Maverick, which had
    wanted to sign Hole]

M: I was, I was being dragged through the labyrinth
    of Radio City. I didn't see it.

CL: I was being dragged to tell Dennis Miller to
    tone it down for me and Drew [Barrymore], not
    to be mean to me and Drew. I used to have a
    crush on him.

M: Why?

CL: Well, I lived here [in New York City]—no, I did—and my friend did the sound on *Saturday Night Live,* and I used to go down to the green room and stare at him. You know, because he was funny and I like funny guys that are smarter.

M: Me too.

CL: I'm so over the rock-star thing. But you don't even do rock stars. As Michael Stipe would say, you dip into the population, right?

M: Yeah.

CL: Yeah, you know, it's like working in the hospital and then going out with the ambulance driver. It's like, "I wanna be a surgeon, I wanna be the top surgeon, dammit, I wanna *own* the hospital!" So I go out with the other surgeons and they're all assholes. So maybe I should try a candy striper.

M: I think you should get out of the hospital.

CL: No, man, I like it in here. Nice clothes . . . good money.

M: And a lot of available drugs.

CL: A lot of available . . . hey, yeah.

M: Anyway, who's got better shoes? Mine are Gucci.

CL: I know they're Gucci.

M: And yours are . . . ?

KL [showing his boots]: Mine were from a baby pony . . .

CL: That sucks!

M: The guys at PETA are not going to like your shoes.

KL: I don't care.

216

CL: That sucks, they're very un-P.C. That's really un-PETA. We can do leather but you cannot do fur. [to Madonna] I went to *Truth or Dare* with Kurt when we were first going out, and he goes, "Jesus, that's *you!*"

M: Really?

CL: I think it was like the part where Warren says, "What doesn't belong on camera?" [While Courtney is still talking, Madonna gets up to leave.]

KL: Well, Madonna's running off. That ended well.

M: Bye.

KL: Well, Courtney, thank you.

CL: I like a good entrance. Was I bumming you guys out? Were you, like, talking astrophysics and stuff? [shouting] Bye, Madonna . . . Did I bum you out? Are you pissed at me? Swear to God?

[Madonna is shown walking away, shaking her head and looking pissed.]

In November, Courtney traveled to Orlando, Florida, to deal with the trumped-up charges of two fans who claimed she'd beaten them up in the mosh pit during a show. Even the judge found this ridiculous, noting that their injuries were no worse than one could reasonably expect to incur at a "punk-rock show." (In March 1997 she would sue Orange County for legal fees of $27,000, some of which had been spent paying a psychiatrist to listen to *Live Through This,* watch a video, and read her *Vanity Fair* profile—the new one.)

In December, she brought her band to New Orleans to write most of their third album. Earlier in the year, Courtney had looked at several houses in the Garden District, and had seriously considered buying one. The fact that Trent Reznor already lived in the Garden District didn't deter her. She had first visited New Orleans with Kurt, and they had both loved the city. She had friends there: novelist Anne Rice, a native New Orleanian; R.E.M. guitarist Peter Buck, who then owned a home in the French Quarter; and members of glam-goth band Marilyn Manson, who invade the city sporadically.

Diverting the press with a claim that they had rented "a mansion across from Anne Rice's" (Rice owns several homes in the city), Hole moved into a house on Louisiana Avenue near St. Charles. A few days after their arrival, Courtney and Patty Schemel were roughed up by backstage security guards while attending a Green Day concert at the UNO Lakefront Arena.

"My arm was grabbed and pulled behind my back," Courtney told the New Orleans *Times-Picayune*. "Then I was pulled by my hair. They kept putting their hands over my mouth. My head was banged one, two, three, four times against a steel pole. While this was happening, one guy was doing things down by my underwear. You don't touch a human being like that, celebrity or not." After they'd dragged her out of the backstage area, "one of them said, 'Oh, you're Courtney Love, I'm sorry, it's all a big mistake.' As if, just because I'm me, I shouldn't have been treated that way, but if I wasn't me, then I should."

Courtney suffered bruises and a cut lip. More worryingly, Patty's wrist was hurt, but the injury turned out to be a minor one.

They wrote some music, had a small fire (in Courtney's room, due to her habit of falling asleep with candles burning), and went out very seldom. Courtney was afraid of seeing Trent, and the others didn't care for New Orleans. By the time they left, just before Christmas, Courtney wasn't sure she still liked the city either. She'd been touched by the dark miasma that hangs over the city, spooked by its voodoo spell. She abandoned plans to buy a house, citing as her reason that New Orleans was a bad place to raise children.

"I want witches and vampires!" she'd told a New Orleans real estate agent back in the spring. Those things might still be all right, but she hadn't counted on so many ghosts.

CHAPTER TWENTY-FOUR

◇

In early 1996, shooting for *The People vs. Larry Flynt* began in Memphis, Tennessee. Courtney had gone on a strict no-carbohydrates diet and lost a tremendous amount of weight for the film. "It was the weirdest diet in the world," she told *Premiere.* "Meat, tomatoes, tuna fish, Crystal Light, Jell-O, egg whites, and soy cheese." Her appearance worried some people, but she shrugged and let them worry; she had to pass for a wasted seven-teen-year-old, so she could hardly look robust.

"If somebody's going to pay me a lot of money to be a hundred pounds and if there's a good reason for it and I'm not promoting anorexia, I'll do it," she would say later. But she also admitted, "When you get that thin you start to feel vulnerable. You've reduced yourself, literally."

Rumors of a long-distance dalliance with Gavin Rossdale, singer for the Nirvana-like Brit-pop band Bush, ended when she and costar Edward Norton became involved. When he left the set to shoot scenes for another movie, she played with Frances and read a lot. Her Memphis bookshelf included biographies of Elizabeth Taylor, Jack Nicholson, Barbra Streisand, Janis Joplin, and Milos Forman, as well as Anne Sexton's *Complete Poems,* Ian McEwan's *First Love, Last Rites,* Peter Straub's *The Hellfire Club,* and not one but two copies of Dr. Laura Schlessinger's *Ten Stupid Things Women Do to Mess Up Their Lives.*

Her diet and another bad habit—simply forgetting to sleep—made for some hard days on the set. For years, and especially since Kurt's death, drugs had helped her sleep. Since she'd gotten clean for the movie, Courtney often went forty-eight hours or more without sleeping. Much of what observers have mistaken for chemical influence on her behavior ("slurred speech," "staggering," etc.), if present, can be attributed largely to sleep deprivation.

All in all, though, the consensus on the set of *Larry Flynt* was that Courtney Love was going to make a great Althea. She wasn't easy to work with, especially if you were in the makeup department, and she sometimes had to be dragged out of the fold-up bed in her trailer. But when she stepped in front of the camera, she caught fire. "When we first started, Courtney knew fuck-all about making movies," said a production assistant. "The first week was, like, 'Uh-oh.' Then after that she got it all down. She knows lighting, camera angles, *everything.*"

The techies loved her ability to pick up cues and timing. Milos Forman, though, loved her sheer electric presence before the camera and her chemistry with Woody Harrelson. In the notes accompanying their book of the film's shooting script, scriptwriters Scott Alexander and Larry Karaszewski commented on her ability to improvise: "Dozens of actresses auditioned for Althea, and they were given [the scene where new stripper Althea meets Larry] . . . the marriage proposal [scene] . . . and [the scene where] Larry tells Althea he's born again. Milos felt Althea was a raw, ferocious character, and he encouraged spontaneity . . . Thus, when it was time for Courtney Love to play these three scenes in the movie, she used her audition versions. Milos wanted crazed realism between Woody and Courtney, so he utilized two cameras, letting them perform in real time. It's not exactly what we wrote, but it is vivid."

Memphis was bitterly cold. The company had housed Courtney, Frances Bean, and Frances' nanny in a cookie-cutter luxury suburb, prefab and evil. One day while they were shooting a scene of an angry crowd protesting at Larry's court appearance, a local TV news crew parked nearby and filmed the filming. That night's news reported that the crowd of extras was actually protesting the movie!

Courtney was glad when the filming moved on to L.A.— until they got to the scenes where Larry and Althea start shooting heroin. The props department had fake hypodermics with retracting needles, fake black tar, everything but the high. She had to inject Woody, then tie off her own vein with rubber tubing, shoot up, and pass out. The scene disturbed her deeply, but Woody and his longtime girlfriend, Laura Louie, helped talk her through it while Frances played with their three-year-old daughter, Deni.

Courtney would spend much of her screen time nude or scantily clad, dancing onstage, frolicking in a hot tub with two women, in bed with Woody.

"Courtney is really going to be a big surprise," Harrelson told *Detour* after the film was wrapped. "She is so good, so in-the-moment, and so real. Milos fought really hard to make it happen with her; he really wanted her. She's wild, man, she is wild. I'll tell you what, if I work another twenty years of my life, I hope to be as good as she is now, on her first big shot. You won't believe how incredible, how riveting she is to watch. I've watched her in the dailies—it's not just speculation. She really is riveting. She's dedicated, and very professional. Sure, she's crazy as hell, but she's also driven and very focused."

He said much the same thing to *Us,* but added a story about going to see *Death of a Salesman* with her. "She'd been up the whole night before, but I didn't find this out till later. She slept from the moment the curtain rose—*before* the curtain rose—until the end of the play. Except she was awake during the intermission . . . Head back, mouth open—and her legs! At the beginning of the second act, her legs would just suddenly go over the seat in front of her and there'd be a big bustle of her [waking up], and then she'd fall back to sleep and they'd go back up. . . . I was *so* anxiety-ridden."

She spent the next couple of months writing more lyrics and traveling with her new boyfriend, Edward Norton. A conservative, media-wary young man, a Yale graduate fluent in Japanese, Norton appreciated Courtney's intelligence more than her wildness. "I think she was really born to play [Althea]," he told *Premiere.* "When you meet people like Courtney who have been culturally iconic in a way that very few people are, you really see the distance between the press's manipulation of a person's image and the reality of that person. There's an enormous amount of loose hyperbole that doesn't take in the complexities of a person's life and personality. Meeting her was a real lesson in that."

In May, the *Seattle Post-Intelligencer* reported that she was tearing down the greenhouse where Kurt had committed suicide because it had become a macabre tourist attraction. Nirvana fans all over the world protested the destruction of "Kurt's house" and vilified Courtney as if she were doing it on a whim. In truth, the city had unearthed old survey documents showing that part of the Love-Cobain property encroached on Viretta Park—specifically, part of the driveway and about half of the greenhouse—and they were demanding the return of the land. Rather than demolishing the building, Courtney had it moved to the other side of the property and refurbished as a guesthouse.

Also in May, someone gave Seattle radio station 107.7 The End a tape of Kurt and Courtney singing a duet of "Asking for It." The tape was from the *Live Through This* studio sessions, during which Kurt had sung backup vocals on several songs. Back in 1995, discussing Kurt's influence on her own music, Courtney had said, "My feeling has always been, put lyrics on top of *every single note.* I learned a lot about space from Kurt, and a lot about harmonies. There are harmonies all over [*Live Through This*] that are Kurt's . . . you can hear him on 'Pee Girl' . . ."

In an unauthorized and unflattering biography of Courtney published in 1996, author Melissa Rossi cited a rumor that Kurt had written most or all of the songs on *Live Through This,* and that a demo tape still existed of him playing and singing them. Courtney's detractors took the "Asking for It" tape as proof of this rumor, even though this version of the song was obviously not from any such demo tape; it was studio-quality.

In fact, this version of "Asking for It" had been recorded because Courtney had hoped to release it as a single, and she knew fans would enjoy hearing her and Kurt together. After his death, she had abandoned the idea.

In July 1996, Hole's cover of Fleetwood Mac's "Gold Dust Woman" appeared on the soundtrack of *The Crow: City of Angels,* and various sources reported that Hole's new album—supposedly titled *Celebrity Skin* because, as Courtney said, "I've touched so much of it"—was being recorded.

Speaking publicly about this album, Courtney described songs about abortions, about self-mutilation, about imagining her own funeral in New Orleans, about rock stars cheating on their wives,

about sex. "It's hard to write about sex," she told *NME*, "and
. . . the Kurt relationship . . . I know exactly how I want it to
sound: I built it in my mind, like a circle. The top end I want to
be warm, Crazy Horse, *Harvest*. The middle strip is really Alan
Moulder, with strong songwriting. Like what Billy [Corgan] did
with *Siamese Dream*, but more so and less so. Textured, supertex-
tured. The bottom part I want to be the gnarliest, Black Sabbath
meets sampling . . . gnarly and deep and hard."

She had her lyrics—she always had her lyrics—but the songs
weren't falling together. In July, Courtney took a break from the
project and checked herself into rehab in Pennsylvania, allegedly
for Valium dependency. The rumor was that Edward Norton had
given her an ultimatum: clean up or break up. As a curious part
of her rehab plan, she moved in with actress Drew Barrymore
when she returned to L.A. Work continued on the album.

Music took a backseat, though, when *The People vs. Larry
Flynt* was released in December 1996. The buzz had been building for months, and Courtney's performance exceeded all expec-
tations. Reviews bubbled over with astonishment and enthusiasm.

"Love's performance is an amazement," reported *Newsweek*.
"Funny, unfettered and almost scarily alive in front of a camera,
she's the definition of a 'natural.'" *Spin* raved, "Her Althea is a
corrosive, silky, sensible whore, and every time Love cracks that
sick smile, the camera swallows her whole." Even Flynt himself
offered grudging approval: "Milos saw something in Courtney
that nobody else saw, and he captured it on film. I was blown
away by her in the movie. Milos got absolute perfection out of
her."

Us claimed that "Love [had] locate[d] the film's grieving heart
without cheap tears and [struck] a note of pure, unvarnished
grace." The *New York Times* declared Courtney "a smashing Althea." *People* pointed out that "[s]he's the only person in this
cheerfully inoffensive film who looks as if she *likes* sex, and the

dirtier the better." She'd garnered a Golden Globe nomination before *Larry Flynt* ever hit the theaters; subsequently she won the New York Film Critics Award, the Boston Film Critics Award, and the Golden Satellite Award for best supporting actress in a major motion picture. Now people were talking about an Oscar nomination. Courtney couldn't believe it—the adults were starting to approve of her.

She began to clean up her image accordingly. The January *Vogue* featured "Courtney Love's Major Makeover": four pages of the star dressed in Versace, Dolce & Gabbana, Alberta Ferretti, and Valentino, saying things like, "I've learned only recently how to do clothes. When I had no money, I did thrift shop, and I always knew exactly what to buy. Then I got money, and I stopped doing thrift shop and started doing mall. I suddenly didn't know what to buy anymore."

When interviewed for the *Today* show, she refused to answer questions about drugs because of the show's "demographic." The host persisted. After determining that the cameras were rolling, an exquisitely polite Courtney stood up and started to walk off the set. She got her way without uttering a single "fuck you."

All these good manners threw the media for a loop. Soon she was making headlines for her "new image," her "cleanup," her "transformation." Of course, it was all seen as a calculated commercial move; no one seemed to consider the fact that she might really be in the process of growing up.

She didn't get the Oscar nomination that the glossy magazines had predicted, but she did appear as a presenter, hair in a neat blonde bob, sleekly clad in a silver Versace gown. And she behaved herself—no girl-kissing or journalist-threatening, as she'd done with Amanda DeCadenet two years ago.

Several months before the event, *Brandweek* asked women across America to list the Hollywood celebrity expected at the Academy Awards whose fashion sense they most respected.

Courtney had placed third on the list. The response (and perhaps the Versace) led the magazine to hail her as a role model, one who had walked through the fire without scorching her couture:

> The understated elegance of Love's [outfit] on Oscar night may have seemed to some a dramatic departure from her grunge look or, worse, a sign of conformity, but nothing could be further from the truth. Her fashion statement was an equally strong and honest voicing of the many sides to her personality. To many women in our survey, Love represents the epitome of honesty, courage and individuality. They respect the way she so confidently expresses herself through her clothing and her appearance. And they believe that she chooses the clothing she wears because it allows her true colors to come through.

Yes, the grown-ups loved her now.

◇

Early in 1997, Courtney put her Seattle house up for sale and

moved with Frances to L.A. After Children's Services had tried

to take Frances away from her and Kurt, Courtney had thought

L.A. would hold too many bad memories for her ever to live

there again. Now Seattle was full of bad memories, and her lover

and most of her friends were in L.A.

She told the press she was selling the property on Lake Wash-

ington because too many kids came to worship at the shrine of

Kurt's death, which was at least partly true. She left Seattle with a clear conscience: she'd repaired her edgy relationship with Krist and Dave, and Frances would be able to fly up and visit Grandma Wendy or Grandpa Frank anytime she wanted.

The house was sold in May, reportedly for close to the asking price of $2.9 million. The buyers were required to sign an agreement promising not to turn the property into a museum or tourist attraction. The agreement also stipulated that, when Courtney settled in L.A., she would be able to come back and take the willow tree beneath which a portion of Kurt's ashes had been buried.

Kurt. Her precious memory, and her curse. Work on the new Hole record wasn't going well. The rumor that Kurt had written *Live Through This* was unfounded, but Kurt had helped her in myriad ways; it would be ridiculous to think otherwise of musicians who lived together for two and a half years.

Her band had become lethargic from doing nothing. Courtney despaired of ever getting the songs assimilated and composed the way she wanted them. She beat herself over the head with her lack of craftsmanship. She was exhausted. And then Billy Corgan called.

Since the end of their relationship, Billy had achieved solid alt-rock fame with *Siamese Dream* and its follow-up *Pisces Iscariot*, but wasn't satisfied with that. In late 1995 Smashing Pumpkins released the epic *Mellon Collie and the Infinite Sadness*, which would go on to become the best-selling double CD of all time. But in 1996 they suffered a setback while touring the U.S.: a keyboard player traveling with them died of a heroin overdose while shooting up with the Pumpkins' drummer, Jimmy Chamberlin. A few days later, Billy announced that Chamberlin would be leaving the band and checking into a rehab center. The Pumpkins hired a new drummer and continued with the tour.

Now Billy was on the phone, saying, in essence, "You know what, I think you're really tired, and I think you really need me, and I'm your friend and I want you to use me to help compose the record."

Never in a million years would Courtney have thought she'd let Billy mess with her music. But he knew her so well. He knew how to say all the right things. And she *was* tired, and she *was* going nuts with the pre-production. She asked him to come.

Billy had become a good piano player, and together he, Courtney, and Eric deconstructed and rebuilt several of the songs she had already written. Part of his task was to change what Courtney called her "communist" attitude toward music, part of Sonic Youth's legacy, the urge to make the good note bad. Billy convinced her that it wasn't wrong to be influenced by the cheesy, catchy, classic pop she'd heard as a kid. "Sit down and listen to E.L.O. if that's what it takes," he exhorted her. "Whatever it is you need to do to embrace the cheese."

Then the rhythm section came in and Billy worked with them too, urging them to confront their own cheese. She'd never seen Eric blossom so much, and even Patty the rock purist put down her drumsticks at one point and said, "God, this is cheesy, but I *like* it!"

"It's *not* cheesy!" Courtney argued. "Or if it is, that's good. You know what? All the music I've ever loved has been feel-good music at some level. You can get a thing out to a lot of people by making it great and pretty and having it transcend persona and baggage."

Billy smiled. As always, she'd taken the core of an idea and run with it, made it totally her own.

Before Billy hooked up with Hole, he and Melissa Auf Der Maur had worked together on a Ric Ocasek album. "Melissa's got the most incredibly cool sense of melody," said Courtney, "but she really is unchained and has gotten by, by being 'cool' and playing 'cool.' But not real craft. So she spent a month working with Billy on Ric Ocasek and came back *educated*. This one song she wrote is great."

231

The album was turning out to be all about California, with one pointed valentine to Seattle. Courtney wanted to call it *Reasons to Be Beautiful*, which seemed to fit well into her trilogy of titles. But Billy suggested they call it *Malibu*. "It's so California, it's so Beach Boys, it's so sick, you really should consider it," he insisted. Courtney liked the idea.

In a way, it felt as if Hole had skipped their third album and gone straight to the fourth. This wasn't *Celebrity Skin* (though Courtney did write a song by that name), it wasn't really about Kurt (after the eerie prescience of the lyrics on *Live Through This*, that seemed pointless), and it was most definitely a post-movie-star record. But not in a jaded way. When she played the demo for Michael Stipe, he praised its lack of cynicism. "Cynicism is evil," Courtney replied.

To remind herself of that, she took Frances to see *Sesame Street Live* the next time they were in New York. Frances watched the show with rapt attention, but when it was over, she lolled nonchalantly in her seat and said, "Can we go backstage now?"

O jaded rock'n'roll child, Courtney thought. Of course they *could* go backstage, and they met Elmo, and the almost-five-year-old child who had met most of the biggest rock stars in the Western world was starstruck.

Frances' other great passion was fairies. When Courtney asked why, Frances explained her feminist theory of fairies: they were all girls, and they didn't ever have to get married if they didn't want to.

Her child was going to be all right. That was the most important thing, and it seemed to be coming true. Courtney had tried to shield Frances as much as possible from the all-too-adoring public. She'd never encountered anyone who wanted to hurt Frances, but young fans in particular would fix the little girl with a hungry, greedy gaze. Frances was very conscious of it, and if it went on too long, she would put her hands over her face and start screaming, *"Awaaaay from meeeeee,"* with all the power of her awesome lungs.

That gaze was vampiric, Courtney thought, literally so; those kids weren't looking at Frances herself, they were looking for her parents in her. Courtney caught herself doing it sometimes. It was difficult not to; Frances looked more like her father with each passing year.

In May, Hole was invited to watch Fleetwood Mac rehearse for *MTV Unplugged.* Courtney was thrilled—the band, and especially Stevie Nicks, represented everything she loved about the glitter-spangled, tacky-glamorous world of pop music. That was why she'd chosen to cover "Gold Dust Woman" on the soundtrack of *The Crow: City of Angels*—to her, Stevie Nicks *was* the Gold Dust Woman.

Of the rehearsal itself, Courtney said, "Even the most jaded people in my band started crying. It was insane. That's the real lesson in the transcendence of popular music. Those three people open their mouths and they sing together and you're in 1977." When she was introduced to the band after the rehearsal, she felt like Frances meeting Elmo, only not as poised.

Billy had tentatively promised to produce the new record, but after the intensity of the time he'd already spent with Hole, he was exhausted. Courtney saw he'd done all he could, and what a great lot that was: she would be grateful to him forever. In June 1997, Hole went into the studio with Michael Beinhorn, who had produced Soundgarden and the Red Hot Chili Peppers but came from a modern classical/ambient background of musicians like John Cage, Philip Glass, and Brian Eno.

"He's not into the credibility thing," Courtney said of Beinhorn, "that bad-note-for-a-bad-note's-sake thing that has destroyed most of my generation as composers . . . I'm so excited about this record, because in its own way it goes through every single thing that I need to address, yet it's still amazingly good . . .

"It's like a spoonful of sugar helps the medicine go down, with the biggest hooks attached to some really nasty stuff."

Which, come to think of it, was a spot-on metaphor for Courtney's life in general.

Rumors of her impending marriage to Edward Norton kept cropping up in the tabloids, but because of Ed's distaste for the media spotlight, they denied their relationship to the press and made a point of mingling separately at events they attended together. Courtney planned to do more acting when she had time, but was committed to her band for the foreseeable future. Edward was busy with his own film work and had very little interest in the rock'n'roll world, which was fine with Courtney. She'd had enough rock-star boyfriends for maybe a couple of lifetimes.

She was reluctant to say she was happy—she feared happiness as a state of stagnation—but her life was more peaceful than it had ever been before.

Could Courtney Love, with her nuclear temper and her penchant for melodrama, allow that peace to last? She hoped so. And this time she was pretty sure she could.

B I B L I O G R A P H Y

I. Books

Alexander, Scott, and Larry Karaszewski, *The People vs. Larry Flynt (The Shooting Script)*. Newmarket Press, 1996.

Azerrad, Michael. *Come As You Are: The Story of Nirvana*. Doubleday, 1994.

Carver, Lisa Crystal. *Rollerderby: The Book*. Feral House, 1996.

Editors of *Rolling Stone*. *Cobain*. Rolling Stone Press (with Little, Brown, and Company), 1994.

George-Warren, Holly, et al., *The New Rolling Stone Encyclopedia of Rock & Roll*. Fireside/Rolling Stone Press, 1995.

Goldman, Albert. *The Lives of John Lennon*. Bantam, 1988.

Humphrey, Clark. *Loser: The Real Seattle Music Story*. Feral House, 1995.

Juno, Andrea. *Angry Women in Rock: Volume One*. Juno Books, 1996.

Karlen, Neal. *Babes in Toyland: The Making and Selling of a Rock and Roll Band*. Random House, 1994.

O'Brien, Lucy. *She Bop: The Definitive History of Women in Rock, Pop, and Soul*. Penguin, 1995.

Raphael, Amy. *Grrrls (Viva Rock Divas)*. St. Martin's, 1995.

Rossi, Melissa. *Courtney Love: Queen of Noise*. Pocket, 1996.

Spungen, Deborah. *And I Don't Want to Live This Life.* Ballantine, 1983.

Wilson, Susan. *Hole: Look Through This.* UFO Music Books Ltd., 1995.

II. *Periodicals*

Allman, Kevin. "The Dark Side of Kurt Cobain." *The Advocate,* February 9, 1993.

Ansen, David. "Naked Ambition." *Newsweek,* December 23, 1996.

Atkinson, Michael. "American Gigolo." *Spin,* December 1996.

Carver, Lisa. "Mary Lou Lord." *Rollerderby,* issue 17, summer 1995.

Cohen, Jason. "Hole Is a Band, Courtney Love Is a Soap Opera." *Rolling Stone,* August 24, 1995.

Cooper, Dennis. "Love Conquers All." *Spin,* May 1994.

Cummins, Kevin. "I Don't Want to Have a Lot of Enemies When I Die." *New Musical Express,* April 29, 1995.

des Barres, Pamela. "Rock & Roll Needs Courtney Love." *Interview,* March 1994.

Dickinson, Amy. "Kurt Cobain's Final Tour." *Esquire,* February 1995.

DuNoyer, Paul. "Courtney Love." *Q,* August 1995.

France, Kim. "Rock-Me Feminism." *New York,* June 3, 1996.

Fricke, David. "Life After Death." *Rolling Stone,* December 15, 1994.

———. "Smashing Pumpkins." *Rolling Stone,* November 16, 1995.

Gliatto, Tom. "The People vs. Larry Flynt." *People,* January 20, 1997.

Grad, David. "Love—That's All He Needs." *New York Press,* May 29, 1996.

Harrison, Andrew. "Love and Death." *Select,* April 1994.

Heath, Chris. "The Art of Darkness." *Details,* April 1995.

Hirschberg, Lynn. "Strange Love." *Vanity Fair,* September 1992.

Howell, Peter. "Cobain-Love Duet Surfaces on Seattle Radio Station." *Toronto Star,* May 15, 1996.

Katz, Alyssa. "Satellites of Love." *Spin,* June 1996.

Kelly, Christina. "Kurt and Courtney Sitting in a Tree." *Sassy,* April 1992.

Lipsky, David. "Junkie Town." *Rolling Stone,* May 30, 1996.

Love, Courtney. "Summer of Love (Lollapalooza 1995 Tour Diary)." *Spin,* December 1995.

Maslin, Janet. "Larry Flynt, His Epiphanies Showing." *New York Times,* October 12, 1996.

Millea, Holly. "True Love?" *Premiere,* February 1997.

O'Neill, Tom. "Woody Harrelson." *Us,* July 1996.

Poneman, Jonathan. "Family Values." *Spin,* December 1992.

Pouncey, Edwin. "Top Hole." *New Musical Express,* September 14, 1991.

Sessums, Kevin. "Love Story." *Vanity Fair,* June 1995.

Spera, Keith. "Singer Courtney Love Says Arena Guards Abused Her." *Times-Picayune* (New Orleans), December 8, 1995.

Sutherland, Steve. "Love Resurrection." *New Music Express,* April 17, 1993.

Travers, Peter. "Oscar's Love Affair." *Us,* January 1997.

True, Everett. "Foreign Orifice." *Melody Maker,* June 8, 1991.

———. "Pretty on the Inside." *Melody Maker,* August 24, 1991.

Turner, Jim. "Sporting Woody." *Detour,* June/July 1996.

Tyaransen, Olaf. "Love Story." *Hot Press,* November 15, 1995.

Weisbard, Eric. "Sympathy for the Devil." *Spin,* February 1996.

Wiederhorn, Jon. "Lollapalooza." *Rolling Stone,* August 24, 1995.

Williams, David E. "Our Man Flynt." *Film Threat,* February 1997.

Wilson, Amy RaNae. "Hole's Patty Schemel." *Deneuve*, December 1995.

Woods, Vicki. "A Labor of Love (Courtney Love's Major Makeover)." *Vogue*, January 1997.

Ziccardi, Donald. "Love: American Style." *Brandweek*, April 25, 1997.

III. Songs and Albums

Bowie, David. "The Man Who Sold the World." Tintoretto Music/Screen Gems–EMI/Chrysalis Songs, BMI, 1970.

Hole. "Retard Girl." Sympathy for the Record Industry, 1990.

———. "Teenage Whore." *Pretty on the Inside*, Caroline, 1991.

———. "Violet," "Miss World," "Plump," "I Think That I Would Die," "Gutless." *Live Through This*, Geffen/DGC, 1994.

Meat Puppets. "Oh Me." *Meat Puppets II*, SST, 1983.

Nirvana. "Come As You Are," "Something in the Way." *Nevermind*, Geffen/DGC, 1991.

———. "Dumb." *In Utero*, Geffen/DGC, 1993.

———. *MTV Unplugged in New York*. Geffen/DGC, 1994.

The Vaselines. "Jesus Doesn't Want Me for a Sunbeam." EMI-Blackwood Music on behalf of EMI Music Publishing Ltd./ Complete Music Ltd., administered by Incomplete Music Inc., BMI, 1987.

About the Author

Poppy Z. Brite was born on May 25, 1967, in New Orleans. She has worked as an artist's model, a mouse caretaker, a stripper, and (since 1991) a full-time writer. She has published three novels, *Lost Souls, Drawing Blood,* and *Exquisite Corpse,* and a short story collection, *Wormwood.* Her work has appeared in numerous publications, including *Rage, Spin,* and *The Village Voice.* She is the editor of the anthologies *Love in Vein* and *Love in Vein 2.* Her novella "Triads," a collaboration with Christa Faust, appears in Douglas E. Winter's anthology *Revelations.* She lives in New Orleans with her husband, Christopher, a chef and food writer.